"I recommend this practical and insightful .... ve their children and seek to preserve their well-being during and after divorce."

—**Hon. Sondra M. Miller**, Retired Justice of the Appellate Division of the Supreme Court, Second Department

"In this book, Lauren Behrman and Jeffrey Zimmerman have given divorcing parents a remarkable resource for 'radical acceptance' of one's former spouse as he or she actually is—the starting point for putting aside attachment to who is right and who is wrong, and instead cultivating the conditions in oneself for doing the best possible job of minimizing conflict and maximizing good parenting. Behrman and Zimmerman translate wisdom from many traditions—psychotherapy, brain science, dialectical behavior therapy (DBT), mindful awareness, and much more into very practical tools and techniques for moving from victimhood toward competency and equanimity. While their book is addressed to parents in high-conflict divorces, the techniques they offer can make the challenges of raising kids in two households easier for every divorcing couple."

—**Pauline H. Tesler**, longtime family law specialist, fellow of the select American Academy of Matrimonial Lawyers, and founding director of the Integrative Law Institute at Commonweal

"*Loving Your Children More Than You Hate Each Other* is a valuable, interactive guide for co-parents caught in the struggles of a high-conflict divorce. Authors Behrman and Zimmerman cover a full range of emotional responses and behavior patterns that hinder co-parenting success. With compassion and wisdom, they offer strategies for detoxifying messages and generating positive alternatives that build bridges toward safety, respect, and cooperation that support everyone in the family."

—**Rosalind Sedacca**, divorce and parenting coach; founder of the Child-Centered Divorce Network

"Expertly weaving contributions from our understanding of the grief process, DBT, mindfulness, and their own extensive work with high-conflict co-parents, the authors provide professionals and parents a guide to healing and building respectful and functional co-parenting relationships, even when they would rather keep fighting. The beneficiaries of this well-organized, practical book are children and building a societal ethic of cooperative shared parenting."

—**Matthew Sullivan, PhD**, founder of Overcoming Barriers,
    a nonprofit organization that provides training and programs
    for high-conflict shared custody; coauthor of *Overcoming the
    Co-Parenting Trap*

"Loving Your Children More Than You Hate Each Other is an easy-to-read, practical guide for parents to reduce conflict and recover from divorce by focusing on the needs of their children. Parents will identify with the emotional challenges that are described and, through meaningful exercises, move into a new, more resilient and centered place. Behrman and Zimmerman walk parents through this recovery process, incorporating vignettes parents can identify with and ideas from brain science, mindfulness, and DBT to develop skills and techniques that reduce anger and build coping. This is a must-read for parents in conflict who want to move on, focus on raising healthy and well-adjusted children, and learn life skills that make them feel like heroes, rather than survivors or victims."

—**Robin M. Deutsch, PhD, ABPP**, director of the Center of
    Excellence for Children, Families and the Law; professor in the
    clinical psychology doctoral program at William James College;
    and coauthor of *7 Things Your Teenager Won't Tell You*

Loving Your Children More Than You Hate Each Other

POWERFUL TOOLS FOR NAVIGATING A HIGH-CONFLICT DIVORCE

LAUREN J. BEHRMAN, PhD

JEFFREY ZIMMERMAN, PhD, ABPP

New Harbinger Publications, Inc.

Distributed in Canada by Raincoast Books

Copyright © 2018 by Lauren J. Behrman and Jeffrey Zimmerman
New Harbinger Publications, Inc.
5674 Shattuck Avenue
Oakland, CA 94609
www.newharbinger.com

Cover design by Amy Shoup

Acquired by Ryan Buresh

Edited by Rona Bernstein

Library of Congress Cataloging-in-Publication Data on file

20   19   18

10   9   8   7   6   5   4   3   2   1   First Printing

We dedicate this book to our children, Jonathan and Sarah, Ali and Rob, Micah, Liza, and Eli; our grandchildren, Abigail, Sophia, and Daniel; Phyllis Channin; and all our parents. You are our inspiration and we love you all dearly. We also dedicate this book to all children whose parents are caught in conflict. We hope to give your parents tools for allowing the light of their love for you to create a family at peace.

Contents

Introduction

Many parents go through a rocky period surrounding a divorce and find that within a few years after a judgment or settlement, they have settled into a new routine, they are focused on parenting their children together, and their emotions have quieted down. We are writing this book for those parents who find themselves caught in a perpetual battle with each other even after the dust of the divorce process has settled. These are the scores of parents we have seen in our offices over the past twenty-five years, often scarred and battle-weary. We are also writing for their children, who can be caught in family-wars that continue for years beyond their parents' divorce. What children need most is the protective cocoon of two adult parents (their primary caretakers) working together to guide them through the choppy waters of this challenging transition in the family. This book offers tools for healing and moving forward to help you manage your emotions and focus your attention on the well-being of your children. We provide a structure for you to hold onto when life feels chaotic and clarity feels hopeless, so that you can come through the storm of the divorce and its aftermath with the strength and vision needed to do the most important job of your life—raise your children with love in a family of peace.

The concepts in this book draw on many different approaches to helping people deal with stress, emotional trauma, conflict, loss, and depression. Some pertain to cognitive, interpersonal, and humanistic therapies, and some originated in non-Western psychotherapy traditions such as Buddhist teachings. Our intent is to give you a diversified set of tools to break the cycle of conflict between you and your former spouse (your co-parent) that plagues you and your children. The tools were developed based on a number of recent advances in our understanding of adult attachment, relationships, and conflict, as well as studies of the brain and nervous system. Some of the tools also come from different psychotherapeutic, skill-building, and psychoeducational approaches, including mindfulness and dialectical behavior therapy, or DBT (Linehan 1993), that help you change your emotional and behavioral responses by shifting the way you think about stress, emotional pain, and relationships.

The philosophy and theory that underlies DBT deserves special mention. This approach focuses on helping people who are in extreme emotional states and having difficulty regulating their thoughts and emotions (Linehan 1993). DBT skills provide a structure and framework to help parents who are in chronic states of high conflict in their interactions with each other, creating an extreme state of distress that threatens their sense of emotional well-being and security. DBT is based on teaching basic psychosocial skills that, in combination, can give you fuller access to what Linehan terms your *wise mind* (Linehan 1993) and what we have called your *centered self*, which we will describe throughout this book.

Our hope is that if you are motivated to break the cycle, you'll be able to harness these tools, and with them you will have the means to stop your own contributions to the cycle of conflict, even if your parenting partner is not buying in. By controlling your own responses to your co-parent, you can maintain your sense of self, stay more centered, and not simply be a victim to the cycle of conflict that may date back to the marital dynamics that were present long before the divorce. If you are not a partner in that dance, the conflict will have nowhere to go, and, like a raging fire without a source of air, it will eventually cool down. Our goal in writing this book is to help you fully separate emotionally, move forward, heal, and be open to a more joyful life ahead.

Like any death, the death of a marriage ushers in a period of grief and mourning that requires a process of healing with a timetable of its own. At the outset of this book, we will help you to look carefully at your own journey through the grief over the death of your marriage and assess where you are in the grieving process. We will ask you to be brutally honest with yourself about whether you have reached a place of acceptance and can envision your life in a new, postdivorce chapter.

Many of you reading this book may find that one or both of you have not fully grieved the loss of your marriage, and, as a result, you are still quite emotionally attached to your co-parent in a way that is unhealthy for you, your former spouse, and your children. You may have finalized a legal divorce but are nowhere near closure and acceptance; consequently, you are in a way still psychologically married, even if that is primarily based on a negative emotional connection. In other words, your legal divorce is final, but your emotional divorce is not. As a result, you may be stuck in a conflict dynamic (or dance, as we often refer to it) that defines your relationship. The dysfunctional dynamic that permeated your marriage may now be fueled with this extra-strength toxicity and escalated by anger, hurt, and disappointment. When you don't fully grieve the loss of your marriage to reach a place of closure and acceptance, you can be hurting your own soul and blocking your own path to emotional healing and growth.

When the conflict persists way beyond the divorce, we believe it takes on the characteristics of an addiction, in which one or both parents seem to have a need to continue the conflict despite the harmful effects to them *and* the children. This *conflict addiction* (Thayer and Zimmerman 2001) maintains the connection between the formerly married partners. When this takes hold, it doesn't matter what the content of the disagreement may be, as anything can trigger an outburst and lead to conflict that binds you and your co-parent together, albeit in a deeply damaging way. When your children are watching this occur repeatedly in front-row seats, their emotional safety and development is challenged.

Are your beloved children being raised by parents who are caught in conflict addiction, where the slightest things lead to one conflict after another? If so, they are at greater risk of emotional, behavioral, and academic challenges. Their memories of childhood and future love relationships are at risk for being spoiled and burdened. Is this the legacy you want to leave them? You have the opportunity to teach them about resilience—that families and relationships can heal and be safe places, and that love, not anger and bitterness, dominates their childhood and future.

Description of This Book

This book is meant as a guide to help you extricate yourself from the cycle of conflict and protect your children, even if your co-parenting partner is not open to sharing in this quest. The chapters in the first section of the book are written to help you as an individual parent understand your emotional responses and how your brain works during conflict, as well as to learn ways to regulate your emotions so you can begin to transform yourself from victim to survivor to hero. In chapter 1 we will educate you about the emotional responses associated with unresolved mourning in divorce and the impact of these emotions on your body, your co-parenting relationship, and other areas of your life. In chapter 2 we will help you understand what happens to your brain when you are in conflict and describe how new brain research has given us insight into the relationship between our emotions and our brain. In chapter 3 we will offer skills and strategies for regulating emotion that come from the literature on DBT, as well as discuss other important concepts such as shame, dignity, compassion, and mindfulness. In chapter 4 we will focus on ways to discover your authentic self and become a survivor and even a hero, rather than a victim. We will look at the opportunities for growth that can emerge from the experience of your divorce and help you shift your own view of yourself and test your commitment to being different in some key ways.

Part 2 will focus on your journey as a co-parent. These chapters will educate you about how to reduce your ongoing conflict, how to create safety in your co-parenting relationship, how to love your children more than you hate each other, and how to recover from your divorce. We will describe how you can let go of your attachment to the past and shift your communication with your co-parent from defensive, critical, and hostile interactions to those that are focused, productive, and aimed at identifying and addressing your children's needs. In chapter 5 we will delve deeply into ideas about conflict and teach you skills for developing distress tolerance when interactions with your child's other parent become stressful. In chapter 6 we will help you reframe your postdivorce relationship from that of a married couple to that of a parental team. We will help you unite around your love and concern for your children and discover how to create safe emotional bonds between you and your co-parent for your children's sake and a sense of shared commitment as a parenting team. We will show you techniques to work directly on your own contribution to the cycle of conflict. In chapter 7 we deepen the discussion to help you incorporate the skills you've learned in chapters 5 and 6 to bond with your co-parent around the Herculean task of parenthood that you began together when your children were born and that will continue throughout your life and theirs, and through future generations, even beyond your lifetime. Chapter 8 will focus on strategies for divorce recovery. We will share the concept we call GRACE, offering a formula for approaching forgiveness and acceptance.

Each chapter ends with a brief summary recapping some of the central ideas along with a list of suggestions. We hope that when you return to the book from time to time, you will recall some of the main points by looking at the wrap-up to each chapter.

A few notes about language: We are consciously defining anyone who is parenting along with a former partner as a *co-parent*, rather than an *ex*, to underline the important parenting role you share forever, even if you are not co-parenting well at the moment. Also, for simplicity, we use the word *children* in the plural to refer to one or more children.

By the way, our use of gender throughout this book does not imply that we are speaking specifically about men or women, boys or girls. Also, we are not limiting this book to heterosexual couples or couples who were legally married. Certainly same-sex marriages and common law relationships end in divorce, and parents and children in these families can be greatly helped when they reduce the conflict.

This book is not designed to address problems of domestic violence. However, we feel the need to mention that if at any time your physical safety or that of your children feels threatened, you must seek help in a safe way and at a safe time, by contacting a trusted friend, relative, counselor, physician, or attorney, or by calling a domestic violence hotline or child protective services (and, in case of an emergency, 911).

Lastly, the names and identifying information of clients have been thoroughly disguised. If you happen to think you recognize someone you know in the examples, it is merely coincidental.

How to Use This Book

Whether you are on your own in the commitment to end the conflict or you have consensus and buy-in from your former partner, you can begin this next step in your journey from wherever you are. You can share this resource with your co-parent, or first develop your own strategy for working toward keeping your children out of the conflict. As long as one of you embraces the idea that ongoing conflict is toxic for your precious children, and you are determined to step out of the conflict dynamic, you have taken a huge step forward.

We hope you use this book as a guide to developing skills and strategies to move away from and beyond the conflict. We recommend that you get a special journal to use as a companion to this book for the numerous exercises aimed at promoting self-reflection and awareness. You can also download worksheet versions of all these exercises on the book's website, http://www.newharbinger.com/39041. (See the very back of this book for more details.) We will teach you to monitor and "scrub" your communications with yourself and your child's other parent so you can write a new chapter of peace for yourself and your children. Let's get started.

PART 1

Your Personal Journey

CHAPTER 1

High-Conflict Divorce and the Emotions of Unresolved Mourning

W hy do some people recover from their divorces and start a new chapter in their lives with the passage of time, while others seem to be stuck in their anger and pain for years and years? We believe that when one or both of you are unable to complete a process of mourning the "death of the marriage," it breeds the resistant strain of conflict we are addressing in this book. In this first chapter, we will look at the stages of mourning, assess where you are in your journey through this grief, and explore what will help you move through the grieving process, if it is not fully completed.

Unresolved grief after divorce leaves you vulnerable to triggers of intense emotion that will have an ongoing impact on your body, your co-parenting relationship, and other areas of your life. Recognizing that highly emotional responses may signal unresolved or unfinished grief is the first step in recovering from the stress and trauma of the divorce. Reaching a healthy acceptance about the divorce will help you create your own stable foundation as you move into building the next chapter of your life.

Why Divorce Triggers Intense Emotion

Divorce is considered by many professionals to be a stressor akin to the death of a loved one. However, we think that in some ways it actually surpasses that level of stress. From an early age we begin to experience mortality. We see relatives and pets die and learn that all life comes to an end. At some level we directly or indirectly prepare for this, and when it happens we mourn, with family, friends, our religious community, and even at times our colleagues supporting us.

However, divorce, while it is frequently described as the "death" of the marriage, is not treated in the same way. To begin, you didn't get married with the clear understanding that your marriage may someday contract a "life-threatening disease." You didn't expect it would end. In fact, to the contrary, you took a solemn vow that only physical death would end the marriage ("until death do us part"). Yet marriages deteriorate, especially when they are given less attention as you deal with careers, children, social commitments, and the demands of building a life together. Day-to-day demands often create distance, pain, and resentment, driving the relationship and feelings away from the warmth and closeness of the past. Each of you may cope in different ways and be vulnerable to betraying the core values that were established during courtship when you repeatedly affirmed your love for one another. As your relationship was ailing, it likely reached a point of no return—where the despair was such that you, your spouse, or both of you contemplated divorce. Most marriages begin to end when one or both spouses come to the realization that they just can't stand the pain in their relationship and have no hope for its recovery. Additionally, while there are many rituals and demonstrations of support from family, friends, and community surrounding the death of a loved one, there are rarely community rituals marking divorce, and often the outpouring of support is not there in the same way. Your own history of losses and your customary ways of coping with stress bear on your resources to mourn and recover from your divorce.

Divorce signals multiple losses. It can threaten to change almost every important aspect of your life. From a change in your most central adult relationship, to changes in time spent with your children, to changes regarding your home, community, finances, lifestyle, friendships, work life, identity as a married person, and even religious affiliations, there is hardly an area of life that divorce does not impact. Throughout the mourning process, strong emotions prevail at different stages. Let's look at the stages of mourning and the emotions associated with them. It's important to note that these stages don't necessarily occur sequentially, and there is often cycling forward and backward through the stages.

Predictable Stages of Mourning

Elisabeth Kübler-Ross (1969) developed a model of stages of grief in dealing with the recognition of impending death. These stages—denial, anger, bargaining, depression or despair, and acceptance—have been expanded upon by clinicians and researchers in psychology and applied to recovering from the death of a loved one, romantic breakups, and divorce. Below we'll describe these stages as they relate to divorce.

The Stage of Denial

The initial stage of responding to a significant loss is described as one of **denial**. In this stage there is numbness and a sense of shock. It is difficult to wrap your head around the idea that the marriage is breaking up. By not facing the ending, you postpone the need to grieve, and you may hold on to an unrealistic hope that the relationship is reparable. Initially the numbness and shock protects you from the waves of emotion, but as the shock wears off, the fear and pain can begin to emerge. Let's look more closely at these two broad emotional experiences.

Fear

With all the life changes that arise around divorce comes a tremendous amount of uncertainty, ambiguity, and fear. These feelings relate to many areas of life and consequently can be very powerful.

Basic needs. On the most core level we have the requirement for food, shelter, health, and clothing. Divorce often impacts some of these, as one if not both partners have to move out of the marital home. The impending financial challenges and unknowns also can threaten one's sense of security. *Where will I live? How will I get by? Will I have enough money for* *my day-to-day expenses? Will I have enough money to take care of the children? How will I save for the children's college expenses and my retirement?*

Job and community. Divorce also threatens the stability in one's daily life. If you work outside the home, you may fear that the divorce and the resulting parenting responsibilities might impact your job security or ability to get promoted. If you do not work outside the home, divorce may mean that you need to deal with the daunting task of managing your childcare responsibilities while entering the workforce for the first time, or reentering after perhaps many years, when your skills may be obsolete. Your social community may change as friends take sides, you feel shame and retreat from relationships, or you need to move from your secular and religious communities. Even your extended family members may distance themselves if they blame you in some way for the divorce. You may also question the impact of these kinds of changes on the children and ask, *How will they adjust to a new school and leaving their friends?*

Given all of these changes, fear is an inevitable component of the first stage of grief. The following journal exercise is aimed at helping you identify your initial fears related to divorce. (As a reminder, you can download this and all the exercises in this book at http://www.newharbinger.com/39041.)

Exercise 1.1: My Fears List

In your journal, please list the fears you had when the thought about divorce or the inevitability of divorce came to your awareness. Make as comprehensive a list as possible.

As you look over the list, you may find you can categorize the fears according to one or more of the areas of basic needs, job, and community we mentioned. You may have also discovered other feelings in your journaling. How strong are these feelings? The stronger they are, and the more they impact you, the more you may benefit from learning specific strategies to address them, which we will discuss throughout this book.

Pain

Whether you initiated the divorce or your partner did, the pain may be categorized in some of the following ways:

Pain resulting from my partner's actions. What betrayals of trust occurred in the marriage around areas such as sex, money, caring, and nurturance? Do you say, *After all I did for the marriage, how could my partner have done this to me?* Blaming your partner for the fall of the marriage is a natural reaction; however, at the same time it makes you a victim and can keep you feeling hurt and angry. We will address this further later on in this book as so many people have difficulty coping with the pain that they view as bestowed on them by their partner.

Pain resulting from my own actions. What are your own contributions to the pain? Are there things you did or did not do that led to the collapse of the marriage? Did some of these actions lead to pain regarding your own sense of self, your core, or your soul? Did your actions toward your spouse betray some of your values? If you initiated the divorce, do you feel a sense of pain or guilt for the havoc this brought on the family? If your partner initiated the divorce, do you repeatedly question what you could have done differently? Some people feel guilty for having endured an unfulfilling or even abusive marriage, saying, *Why did I stay so long?* or *How could I have been so stupid to put up with that?* At some point you may be able to forgive your partner, but can you learn to forgive yourself? That is often more difficult.

Your children's pain. Looking at our children in pain can be more disturbing than looking at our own pain. This *vicarious pain* (the pain we have from seeing someone else in pain) can add a dimension to the divorce that at times seems unbearable, as when we have to stand by and watch our children tolerate a painful medical procedure. How many parents would rather go through that themselves than have their children endure the procedure? That would be easier to take. Unfortunately, in divorce you also have to contend with the pain you see in your children that seems to be the result of what their other parent does or doesn't do. How that parent treats them, differences in parenting styles, and even what the children tell you the other parent said about you can all contribute to your vicarious pain as you see your children more tormented than you may be able to stand.

To identify the particular sources of your pain, please complete this next exercise.

Exercise 1.2: My Pain List

List the sources of emotional pain related to your divorce by answering these questions: Where does your pain come from? How much comes from the present loss? From loss of trust? From betrayal? From your past experiences? From worry about your children? You may find that your pain is primarily from one source, or perhaps it is from many. Often, the more sources it comes from, the greater the intensity of the pain.

The Stage of Anger

The next stage in the mourning process is **anger**. While your initial feelings following the onset of a divorce may be dominated by anxiety and fear of the unknown, at some point the feeling of anger sets in. This anger may be directed at your co-parent, at yourself, at the situation, or possibly at the world. The anger allows you to begin to stand up for your own needs and understand that perhaps you were treated poorly or unfairly and deserve better treatment. The anger can empower you to mobilize your resources and begin to look toward your future. Being able to access the anger is a sign that you are moving through the stages of grief, and it can help you begin to make some changes and be proactive in creating a life that doesn't revolve around this marriage.

While anger can be helpful, it can also be destructive and sabotage your adjustment, so it's important to better understand this emotion. Anger is often a reaction to feeling victimized, taken advantage of, or hurt. In a life-threatening situation, it can be mobilizing and move you to action. Unfortunately, in divorce it can paralyze your recovery and keep you locked into conflict. Your anger may take the following forms:

Anger at Others

It generally is quite easy to get in touch with anger at others. For example, you can see what your partner did and didn't do that you believe led to the collapse of the marriage. You may easily get support for being angry at your partner by talking to friends and family who may readily say, "I can't believe what [name of your partner] did to you. That's unbelievable. You shouldn't let him get away with that." Your anger toward your partner may be exacerbated by the words and actions of the lawyers. Your lawyer may complain about your spouse's lawyer, and you can see that the attacks from your spouse's lawyer are dominated by misrepresentations of your view of the facts, your co-parent's claims and perceptions, motions that are filed, and unreasonable proposals that are being made.

Anger at others can lead to a sense of justifiable retribution, which fuels battles large and small (from fights on the playground to wars between countries). Generally, both sides feel hurt and then react to their own sense of pain and resulting anger. They then attack the other with a certainty that they are in the "right" and justified, having to defend their position and principles. Unfortunately, in families, this anger can lead to perpetual conflict between the parents and to a loss of focus on their children, for example when parents fight over the time of a doctor's appointment or who is at fault in any scenario, rather than focus on and problem solve how to take care of a child's need.

Anger at Self

Anger at oneself is more complicated. As hard as it is to forgive the other person, it is generally harder to forgive ourselves. We will discuss this in more depth later on, but if you were the perpetrator of some wrong against the other person (for example, if your list of pain in exercise 1.2 includes statements such as "Why did I...?" or "Why didn't I...?"), who is there to forgive you? You may view yourself as the wrongdoer and the wronged at the same time. Many times anger at ourselves can complicate the sadness and grief and actually shift it into a clinical depression (particularly when the grief is not resolved). Letting go of this anger can be key to helping you adjust to the divorce and be happier. Inability to let go of anger is often at the core of unremitting conflict.

Let's take a look at your anger.

Exercise 1.3: My Anger List

Please write about your anger in your journal. Who are you angry at? How deep is the anger? Write about how the anger gets triggered and how it helps or hurts your recovery and ability to move past the divorce. Notice too how you feel about the anger. What other thoughts and feelings are triggered when you write about the anger? Anger doesn't exist in a vacuum. It can be connected to many other thoughts, feelings, and behaviors.

The Stage of Bargaining

In the **bargaining** stage, you think of every possible way you could have avoided this outcome, taking full responsibility for the demise of the relationship. You begin to think of what steps you could take to reverse the process, you ask yourself questions like *What if I had done this, or not done that?* and you think, *If only I could have a chance to do something differently.* After all, if you "broke it," you should be able to "fix it." You may promise to fix everything that you have done wrong, attempt to repair the relationship at all costs, and beg to try again. It is painful to face the thought of life without your partner. The future is completely unknown, and that is frightening for most of us. Bargaining can give you the illusion of control, but it often leaves you in the position of having the reality of the divorce crash down on you over and over again.

This next exercise will help you identify your own attempts at bargaining.

Exercise 1.4: My Bargaining List

Think about whether you experienced a stage of bargaining during your divorce process. What can you remember about how you felt at that time? Write your recollections in your journal. Do you still find yourself thinking of ways you could have avoided the breakup of your marriage? Looking back at this time, do you recall being preoccupied with thoughts of how you (or your co-parent) could have prevented this outcome? Bargaining can take many different forms and can connect to your feelings about your actions and your co-parent's. Think about the ways bargaining affected you in your own process. In the early stages of grief following a breakup, bargaining can give you hope and buy you some time in adjusting to life without your partner. If bargaining persists for a long period of time, you can thwart your own ability to move forward. Do you recognize either of these in yourself? What else do you recognize about your experience with bargaining?

The Stage of Depression or Despair

In recognizing that the divorce is inevitable, a stage of **depression or despair** emerges. The primary emotion during this stage is one of sadness and grief.

Grief

Grief is often a response to real and imagined loss. What have you lost? What is now missing? What dreams were not realized? You may find that your grief falls within the following areas:

Grief about what was lost. Perhaps some of the most pronounced losses revolve around what you had in the marriage that has eroded. Is it the feeling of love and safety, being appreciated, being funny? Is it the loving look from your partner that was present when you were dating (and that now maybe has shifted to looks of anger or disdain)? Is it the touch and holding? Or, are the losses more tangible, perhaps relating to loss of a home and other things impacting your lifestyle? Or, is it all of the above?

Grief about what could have been. Some people also grieve the things that could have been as they think about the relationship they imagined having, how it would have felt being married at the weddings of their children and births of grandchildren and what it would have been like growing old together. They may grieve what could have been if only they or their spouse had done something differently. Perhaps you grieve what could have been if you or your co-parent had gone to therapy individually, or together. Or, perhaps there is grief about what could have been if one or both of you had not worked such long hours and you had instead taken more vacations together or had a more romantic marriage. Grief about what could have been can be a very powerful force as you mourn the loss of your dreams.

Grief about the process of divorce. Some couples vow to divorce with peace and to not go to "war." They promise to work closely with one another and to always co-parent in a fair and responsible fashion. They promise that as parents they will always love and be there together for their children, making this promise to the children as well. Did you make some of these vows and promises? What happened when the legal system got involved? Often, one thing leads to another and the injuries leading up to the psychological divorce are now compounded by injuries that occurred during the legal divorce, as the accusations, distortions, violations of privacy, and ultimatums that often accompany litigation cause more pain and grief.

Identifying the particular sources of your grief may help you move through the grieving process.

Exercise 1.5: My Grief

Please describe what grief and sadness you feel or felt about the end of your marriage. How does this impact you? What areas of your life are or were changed because of the grief? When you have completed this journal entry, try to assess how much the grief continues to impact your life, or whether you feel you have come through it. If you have unresolved grief, life may seem to have lost its vitality and color. It can be difficult to see the promising future ahead. If you experience a high degree of conflict in your divorce, you may not have moved through this stage of grief.

The Stage of Acceptance

A milestone in the process of grieving the end of a marriage comes when you begin to envision the future without your spouse and believe that you can be okay and whole in this new chapter of your life. This allows you to move forward and maintain some hope and optimism for your future. In this stage, **acceptance**, you may begin to experience a sense of clarity and a feeling of relief.

Clarity

When you move into acceptance, you can feel a deep awareness that your marriage to your co-parent was not "meant to be." This was not the "love of your life" (even if you thought so at the start). Clarity may take the form of knowing what you need in a relationship, or knowing whether you even want to have a romantic partner in the near or distant future. Clarity can bring a sense of feeling anchored and secure.

Relief

Accompanying many of the above emotions can be a sense of relief. This is not something to feel guilty about, but rather something to pay attention to. The relief can indicate why, in the long run, the divorce might actually be something that is better for you than if the marriage continued as it was. Perhaps you notice some of the following:

The loss of pain. Relief and adjustment to divorce can bring with it the loss of pain. We do not need to endlessly endure pain to build character or prove something to the world. In fact, some would argue we have a right or duty to our children and ourselves to take the opportunity to be happier. The loss of pain can lead you to smile more and be more available and accessible to your children, being able to feel and see the blessings (not just the responsibilities and work) they bring you.

New opportunities and hope. Your relief can also bring with it hope and opportunity for a better future. What did you learn from the divorce? Are you able to identify the childhood wounds that you and your partner brought into this relationship? Do you find yourself attracted to partners who don't activate those wounds? What kinds of relationships are important to you at this point in life? What can you now teach your children about relationships? The Hindus speak of reincarnation happening across lifetimes. However, another way of looking at this is to consider the different lives we can have in this lifetime. Different "chapters" of your life can feel like different lives. Divorce can bring with it the opportunity to start a new chapter. Some people, though, feel guilty about this hope and "new life" as they move forward, as if there is something wrong with being happier. We believe that an opportunity to be happier is not something that is morally wrong. It is not selfish, as long as in the midst of your relief you continue to regard (and don't disregard) the other people who are important to you.

The following exercise is aimed at reflecting upon your own level of acceptance, or lack thereof. To fully explore this, it is helpful to consider your movement through the other stages of grief as well.

Exercise 1.6: Early Recovery

As the marriage comes to an end, or now that it has ended, what is better for you? Is this a surprise? What emotional pain is relieved (like a toothache that is now gone)? How is life better? How might life be better? Please jot the answers to these questions in your journal.

Now, look at all the stages of dealing with the loss of a marriage—denial, anger, bargaining, depression or despair, and acceptance—and examine where you see yourself at each stage. Do you see yourself as having reached a stage of acceptance, or do you find yourself stuck in one of the earlier stages, perhaps in anger, or depression or despair. If this is the case, you have now identified important information about yourself that you can begin to address. Ultimately, we hope this will help you find a way to move to a stage of acceptance and free yourself from conflict with your co-parent.

As you progress though the stages of mourning, you are likely to experience reduced conflict with your co-parent, which can lead to emotional changes. It can also lead to physical changes due to the impact of prolonged emotional stress on the body.

The Impact of Emotions on the Body

Emotions take a toll on our bodies. We can get more fatigued from stressful situations than from hard physical work or exercise. While some physical symptoms result from prolonged stress, other symptoms occur in response to sudden and intense emotional problems. Certainly if you have many of the signs described below, or if they are very intense or have a significant impact on your functioning, we suggest that you see a mental health professional or your doctor for a consultation.

Signs of Depression

The emotional response to the stress of divorce can cause physical symptoms that can actually be associated with a clinical depression. This is beyond what would be considered normal grief and mourning associated with almost any major loss. Symptoms of a clinical depression can include a significant change in your weight, energy, sleep, and concentration, as well as suicidal thoughts. Depression can cause problems in other areas such as drug and alcohol use, physical problems due to inactivity, and even accidents and falls due to decreased concentration. Depression can keep you from doing the things that are important to you and can make it harder to deal with the typical challenges of being a parent. It also can cause the usual frustrations and challenges not related to divorce to have a greater negative impact on you. Depression is not the result of being weak or not trying hard enough to cope with all you have been through. It is not your fault and not caused by the choices you have made; rather, it is a medical condition that requires treatment by a mental health expert.

Signs of Anxiety

We have discussed how divorce creates a sense of havoc in so many areas of your life. It is normal to worry about what the future holds for you. However, the worry and stress can lead to more substantial symptoms of anxiety. Common physical symptoms include chest pain or discomfort, abdominal discomfort or diarrhea, difficulty breathing, shortness of breath, hyperventilation, and dizziness. Other symptoms can include a sense of foreboding or dread, as well as nightmares and difficulty sleeping. Anxiety can also cause irritability and decreased concentration, possibly leading to disturbances in your relationships and your productivity at work. Like depression, anxiety is a treatable condition, so a consultation with a mental health expert is recommended if you are experiencing these symptoms.

The Impact of Emotions on Co-parenting

How have your emotions impacted your relationship with your children's other parent? What are your triggers? In other words, what sends you into a tizzy or leads to your acting in a way that you regret and is not aligned with your true authentic self?

The impact of the emotions around divorce on the co-parenting relationship are many and can be quite profound. As we mentioned in the introduction, we believe this can lead to what has been termed *conflict addiction* (Thayer and Zimmerman 2001), when even the simplest of parental decisions become major sources of conflict. Like any other addiction, conflict addiction can severely impact your children and their family experience. The categories of responses described below relate to our hardwired reactions to sudden stress. Here, we relate them to divorce and how you or your co-parent may react to one another. This can give you a general framework for labeling some of the behaviors you see, which ultimately can help you make a shift in your responses.

The Fight Response

This is perhaps one of the most common responses to threat or stress. It occurs in humans as well as other species. In divorce situations, the *fight response* is seen in the persistent arguments of parents, who often expend a great deal of energy that far exceeds the importance of the argument in the first place. These arguments may involve attempts to prove a point or issues that need resolution. You may argue about the principle or history around an issue, often spoiling a decision you might otherwise agree on if you did not engage in the fight. One or both of you might "dig in" and not budge on an issue, possibly feeling as though you are asserting yourself for the first time. You may fight as you try to teach each other a lesson, as if blaming or being critical might just change your co-parent this time (when it has not in the past). The fight might be about accountability, who is right, or what the "punishment" should be for some perceived violation of the parenting plan (such as arriving early or late to pick up or drop off your child). We have even seen the fight response lead to a child not getting medicine as the parents fought over who was responsible for getting the medicine from one house to the other. The fight response can lead to a lot of energy being spent on arguing and continuing the battle of the divorce.

The Flight Response

The *flight response*, on the other hand, is about not responding to your co-parent. It is the actual statement or the behavior that says, "I'm not going to engage with you. Go pound sand." It can take the form of avoiding discussions; not answering calls, emails, or texts; not responding to requests made by your co-parent; not sending information to your co-parent; and so on. We have seen the flight response lead to a mother being unaware that her children were fighting in the basement because she was outside and did not answer a phone call from the father. The father, it turns out, had called to tell her that he had heard from the children that they were fighting.

The Freeze Response

A less known reaction, the *freeze response*, can be described by the common expression of "a deer in the headlights." This response—becoming immobilized for a time before responding—is also a natural reaction to sudden, unexpected stress. This immobilization can take the form of your mind "going blank," not having words to say, or even being unable to move for a brief time. If your former spouse harshly confronted you when you did not expect it, you may have experienced the freeze response.

In fact, the fight, flight, and freeze responses can be viewed as different forms of hostility or defensiveness, and thus as contributing to conflict. Fight is more overt and active. Flight is more covert and passive. Freeze prevents you from responding in a healthy and timely fashion. None of these bring peace or resolution and often in some ways are a reenactment of what happened in the marriage or what we term the *marital dynamics.* You and your co-parent may sometimes be in the same mode and at other times be in different modes. In chapter 2 we will be discussing what is happening in your brain when you react to perceived threats of danger with a fight, flight, or freeze response.

The Impact of Emotions on Other Areas

Unfortunately, we are not made of separate compartments or cubbies that would keep our emotional reactions from affecting other parts of our lives. But if we were to look at the different areas of our lives as compartments, we would view them as being separated by screens or mesh, rather than concrete, steel, or wood. Things that impact us in one area can easily spill over or through into another area, just as sitting in terrible traffic or having a bad day at work can impact how you behave later at home with loved ones. See how many of the areas below are also impacted by the emotions surrounding your divorce.

Parenting

This is one of the most vulnerable areas, one in which your emotions can have a negative impact far too often. Some parents find they just can't shield the children from the pain they feel about the divorce. They demean the other parent, look depressed and forlorn, overindulge their children (perhaps due to guilt about the divorce), or become short-tempered and strict. Have you found that you are less emotionally available to your children? Or, perhaps you are less tolerant of your children just being children. It can be really difficult to be supportive to a child who complains he was not invited to a friend's house when your own life seems to be coming apart at the seams. Limit setting can also be difficult if you are down in the dumps and simply don't have the strength to fight the battle about electronics or cell phone use once again, especially after the battles you fought earlier in the day about child support, the parenting schedule, or whether you will have to move. At times, a child's actions, demeanor, and even face or body type are reminiscent of that of

24

the other parent. In these cases it can be far too easy to fall into the marital dynamic with that child as your reactions become more reflexive, inadvertently treating him more like your co-parent than your child.

Extended Family and Friends

Sometimes known as the Greek chorus, friends and family can take sides. They can be judgmental and can say and do things that feel like additional wounds and betrayals of your trust in them. They can criticize you for what you do and do not do, and they may not "always be there for you" as they promised. They may not understand the private and hidden elements of the marriage that led to the divorce (nor do you necessarily want to share these with them). Here, too, you may not have the strength to always be supportive to them, given your own pain. You may even find that you feel brittle and easily upset by things that would not have upset you previously. Feeling emotionally raw can cause you to shut down, withdraw, or even overanalyze and overinterpret the actions of people you have felt close to and have cared about or loved for years. This can change the balance of the relationship and lead to even more loss, as key relationships (for example, with in-laws or friends) become more distant or even evaporate. Familiar relationships in your community may also change if you have to move, leave a house of worship, or feel unwelcome at clubs and community centers you belonged to when you were married.

Work

You're stressed. Throughout the day you see emails from your attorney and your spouse on your smartphone. The divorce is buzzing around your head, but you are trying to work. What happens to your concentration, your tact, and your rate of making errors? They can all go in the wrong direction, leading to complications at work. These can be intensified by even the practical problems associated with living without your partner. Before the separation, if your child was sick or needed to go to the doctor, you might have coordinated with the other parent and it would not have been evident at work. Now, perhaps the coordination is reduced, you are picking up what is falling through the cracks, and you are less available at work. Are you also less tolerant of the stresses at work? It's hard to care about whether an order went out a day late or paperwork is filed on time when your life seems to be falling apart.

The Legal Process

Have you made decisions in the legal process out of anger, guilt, spite, hurt, and revenge? Most people probably have. We have seen people spend thousands of dollars fighting over a utility bill of about $150. We have seen forensic custody evaluations conducted because the parents could not decide where the children would sleep one night in a two-week parenting plan cycle. Emotions can easily spill into the legal process, lengthening it, causing it to start up again with additional motions being filed after the divorce is finalized, and impacting you and your children. Letting your emotions color your decision making can be costly and keep you locked in the conflict. It can also lead you to give up your share of the influence over the decision regarding a dispute, as the court's decision is not at all influenced by the logic, love, and knowledge *you* bring to the issue about your children and their well-being. This of course is a big price to pay for the emotions leaking through into the legal process.

Future Relationships

The pain and the need for comfort and security can lead some people to run headlong into the next relationship, not taking the time needed to heal, ignoring the warning signs that there might not be a great fit in the next relationship, and perhaps even putting oneself at risk in terms of personal safety. By not taking the time to assimilate and learn the lessons from your first relationship, you may be vulnerable to choosing a new partner with whom you repeat the same dynamic. On the other hand, the need to avoid pain can cause you to reject potentially supportive partners to try to stay emotionally safe. If you are in a relationship, the emotions of the divorce can lead you to be hypersensitive to the glitches that may be normal in any relationship. You may also tend to spend too much time telling stories of the old relationship to your new partner, who may be unable to see you as anything but a person who is still not "over" the prior relationship. Your emotions also can lead you to react in a more pronounced way to your perceptions of the other person, perhaps even affecting your ability to convey understanding and empathy. The new relationship can even start to feel like a "repeat performance" of the marital dynamic.

Clearly, the emotional response to divorce is one of the more profound, long-lasting, and pervasive experiences imaginable. It can seem as if there are tendrils that reach into almost every corner of your life. As you learn to recognize and deal with the emotions of your divorce, you can truly move away from "hating each other" and move toward the most special and unique relationships in your life—"loving your kids." As you move through the rest of this book, we will show you how to better understand these emotions, see your options, and choose your responses in ways that can help reduce conflict and its impact on you and your children.

Wrapping It Up

In this chapter, we equated divorce to the death of a marriage. We put forth the idea that people who remain in high conflict often have not fully grieved their divorces, and, although they are legally divorced, they may not be emotionally divorced. To reach a place of acceptance, you must fully grieve the divorce. As with a death, grief related to divorce goes through stages identified by Kübler-Ross (1969), with each stage marked by predominant emotions. These emotions have an impact on other areas of your life, on your body, and on your co-parenting relationship. Fight, flight, or freeze reactions—instinctive responses to a feeling of threat or danger—further compound the grieving process. These will be described more fully in the next chapter, where we explain how the brain operates when in constant conflict.

Use the following tips to make the most of what you learned in this chapter.

Taking It Home and Making It Yours

* Take stock of where you are in mourning your divorce. If you see yourself as still stuck in anger or grief, find a counselor, support group, or other resource to help you move to the next stage.

* Recognize the emotions you are holding. Can you use them in positive ways to create something new or support your growth?

* Use your journal as a tool for self-reflection. Write your thoughts, insights, doubts, and questions as they come to you. Don't edit them or worry about spelling and grammar. Just let your inner self have a voice in your journal.

CHAPTER 2

Understanding Your Brain in Conflict

In chapter 1, we described the stages of grief, the emotions associated with those stages, and what the fight, flight, and freeze responses look like for parents in high conflict. In this chapter, we will explain what is happening in your brain when you are taken over by these basic responses, which originate in the brainstem, and then react to your co-parent in one of these ways. We will describe how your brain functions when you're in conflict. Being aware of these phenomena can help free you from the grip of conflict and repair ruptures in your co-parenting relationship.

Your Brain in Fight, Flight, or Freeze States

The fight, flight, or freeze responses are biologically hardwired in humans as a response to perceived threat or danger. These responses are controlled by our brainstem working with the amygdala, a primitive brain structure that evolved over two million years ago. The amygdala is actually two small structures, each the size and shape of an almond, that are part of the limbic system. The amygdala scans our environment for threats to our safety and well-being as it, in a sense, searches for "lions and tigers and bears" and interprets whether what we perceive is a threat.

If it senses a threat, whether real or not, the brainstem prepares our bodies to act.

Exciting new discoveries over the last twenty years about brain functioning are directly applicable to the dynamics of parents in high conflict. Understanding how our brains function can empower us to turn crises into growth opportunities.

The Three-Part Brain

We can think of our brains as being composed of three major areas, also described as the *triune brain*, or three-part brain. In order to visualize the relationships among these three parts, we can use the symbolism of the "hand model of the brain" (Siegel 2012, 21). If you fold your thumb over your palm and curve your fingers over your thumb in a kind of fist, you can represent a three-dimensional model of your brain. In this model, your fingers symbolize the outermost area, or covering, of the brain, which is called the cortex. This is the seat of thinking, reasoning, and perceiving the outside world, also known as our higher-level mental functions. Sitting underneath the cortex is the limbic area, which is represented by our thumb. This part of the brain is processing our emotions, motivations, memory, attachment relationships, and how we attribute meaning to our experiences: What is the significance of an event? What is the outcome and consequence of an experience? How do we understand or make sense of something? What is the truth of something? In the palm of our hand would be the most primitive area of the brain, the brainstem, where the fight, flight, or freeze survival reactions to threat are activated. This part of our brain also regulates basic body functions such as heart and respiration rate (Siegel 2012).

The cortex, or covering of our brain, has different areas that are responsible for different functions. One area, the prefrontal cortex, links the three areas of our brain to each other and regulates input from them as well as from our bodies and the outside world, allowing us to be in balance with our bodies and the other people in our lives—our family, friends, coworkers, and others we come in contact with. This is the thinking, reasoning, and problem-solving part of our brain. However, when we are in a state of high alert and taken over by our primitive brain structures (sometimes called the *monkey brain*), we can "flip our lids" (imagine the hand model of the brain once again, and suddenly raising the fingers that cover the thumb and the palm) and lose access to our sound minds. In these moments we are operating without flexibility in our responses, insight into ourselves, rational thought, and possibly even emotional balance, empathy, and morality, as if we are on autopilot.

Flipping Our Lids, and Taking the Low Road or the High Road

In our most recent presidential campaign, we saw many demonstrations of "taking the low road," and we also heard the slogan "When they go low, we go high." This is a good mantra for parents in high conflict.

What is the low road and what happens when we take it? When we go directly from a triggered state in our limbic system into action and speech without thought, we are likely to impulsively say and do things that are critical and harsh and hurt our relationships. We call this "taking the low road." Our words and deeds are not subject to our thoughtful and rational minds, as we have bypassed our higher-level brain functioning. Daniel Goleman (1995) coined the term *amygdala hijack* to describe what happens in these moments when we flip our lids and act in ways that rupture our relationships. In these moments of amygdala hijack, it's almost as if we lose 50 IQ points and aren't able to think, act, or make any decisions in a rational way. Without having the training for how to override your fight, flight, or freeze response, we are at the mercy of our primitive monkey brain in these critical moments and are likely to take the low road. However, when we recognize that we are emotionally triggered and we pause for a moment before we speak and act, taking the time to think through a measured and considered response, we can prepare to take the high road.

Think of a pilot and a copilot flying a plane at 30,000 feet when an engine catches on fire. They can fight and blame each other about whose fault it was, who checked the engine last before they took off, and who should have been keeping an eye on that gauge on the control panel so they would have caught it before it became a problem. Or, they can flee by saying to the other, "I don't want to deal with it; you deal with it" or by running out of the cockpit screaming into the cabin, "There's an engine on fire! There's an engine on fire!" Or, they can freeze and simply sit paralyzed, saying, "Oh my God, there's an engine on fire." However, fortunately, they can override the brainstem response and rely on their higher-level brain functioning to go through the protocols they've over-learned and practiced many times for how to deal with this emergency situation. In other words, they can take the high road. So even though they are scared and anxious, they take the steps they need to land the plane safely at the nearest airport.

Now let's apply this to your own life.

Exercise 2.1:
Understanding My
Emotional Response

(Remember, you can download this and all the exercises in this book at http://www.newharbinger.com/39041.)

Think about your own experience of having a reactive emotional outburst. What physical sensations do you experience in those moments? When you are activated in this way, are you a person that tends to fight, flee, or freeze? Do you tend to react the same way in all emotionally charged situations, or do you find yourself having different reactions in similar situations when you are with people other than your co-parent? Write about your experiences in your journal. See what common threads you can find when you look at a number of times you were emotionally activated.

The Anatomy of an Amygdala Hijack

As you read in chapter 1, often marriages end with a great deal of hurt, anger, betrayal, and loss of trust. Lifelong dreams may be dashed and emotions may run high. When you've faced other losses in your past, perhaps even the divorce of your own parents when you were a child, you may be dealing with multiple layers of loss and grief. Our legal system often fans the flames of conflict as two parents become legal adversaries and fight bitterly over children and money. These factors create the conditions that prime parents to be easily overtaken by amygdala hijacks and fight, flight, or freeze reactions. If you've had your trust shattered at the end of a relationship, or lived through a brutal legal battle, you can become traumatized. Your physical systems that mobilize the body to be on high alert, prepared to meet a life-threatening challenge, are set in motion. In these stressful situations, adrenal glands secrete high levels of a hormone called cortisol. This can be adaptive as a short-term approach to dealing with stress, but it becomes problematic when you are in an ongoing, overwhelming situation and a chronic state of preparedness. When your cortisol level is continually high, as can be the case if you are in high conflict during and after divorce, even minor stressors can trigger a fight, flight, or freeze reaction.

Daniel Siegel likens our internal mental world to "an inner sea that is filled with thoughts, feelings, wishes and dreams and hopes" (Siegel 2010, loc. 108). There can also be a "dark side" of "fears, sorrows, dreads, regrets, and nightmares" that can threaten to crash in on us. Living in a state of perpetual high conflict with your children's other parent can activate that stormy internal sea where the winds are high and the water is churning furiously. When you're stuck in the conflict with your co-parent, the slightest look, body language, words, or behaviors can be interpreted as an intentional provocation and can escalate into a major breakdown (going off course into conflict), often in the presence of your children. The experience of being in a chronic high-conflict relationship is in some ways comparable to that of a soldier in a war zone like Afghanistan: a constant state of high alert punctuated by moments of sheer terror. In this chronic state of high alert, it is not unusual that a word, gesture, or expression can be easily misinterpreted as a threat to your basic physical or emotional safety. In these moments you're easily taken over by an amygdala hijack and resort to fighting with your co-parent, fleeing from the interaction, or freezing in a moment of utter helplessness or paralysis.

Case Study of an Amygdala Hijack

When parents are in a conflict dynamic, even everyday situations, like who picks a child up from school or schedules a doctor's appointment, can seem like a train wreck waiting to happen. Other situations are so fraught with emotion by their very nature that the inevitable meltdown (amygdala hijack) is predictable to those who are not caught up in the drama. This was the case when Zach and Cara were in the midst of a task that was emotionally difficult. Already divorced and living apart, they were in the process of dealing with making health decisions about their seriously ill family dog. The two had planned to tackle a difficult parenting problem later that afternoon—consulting with a pediatric endocrinologist together to gain more of an understanding of their son's juvenile diabetes and how they best could manage it in both of their homes. Each parent had a different take on the best way to approach the problem and what kind of protocol to follow, and each blamed the other for not being on top of the child's needs. Even making the plan to go to the endocrinologist together and choosing a provider had required a great deal of work and time.

Zach and Cara had managed to stay focused on their dog's illness until Zach raised a subject that provoked Cara. He insisted that his girlfriend attend their son's basketball tournament the coming weekend. Cara tried to explain that she wanted there to be no stress for Harry during his tournament, and she asked that his girlfriend not attend the event this time. Zach became enraged and blurted out, "My child support payments make it possible for the children to attend activities, and I'm not going to have my girlfriend left out." Cara tried to explain her view that it wasn't about leaving his girlfriend out, but rather about making sure there was no conflict during the tournament that might distract and upset Harry and prevent him from playing his best. She wanted him to have good memories of his sports event. In making her case, she said, "Your girlfriend isn't a mother, and she doesn't understand the feelings of our child." At that, Zach became even more enraged and impulsively spit out, "I'm going to make her pregnant, and then she'll be a mother, so there!" Both provoked, the conflict escalated and the conversation went further and further off track. All of the alarms went off, and a total parental breakdown was set in motion. Any hope of a productive consultation later that day went out the window, and in fact, during their consultation with the endocrinologist, Zach became angry and walked out of the room. The careful plan they had worked on together for the common goal of addressing their child's diabetes was undermined. Everybody lost in the end.

What might have helped avoid the amygdala hijack here? Should Zach and Cara have realized that they were emotionally activated and in conflict? Should one of them have said, "Let's talk about the basketball tournament later?" The next section may give you some answers to these questions.

Learning How to Break the Cycle of Conflict

The first step in learning how to break the cycle of conflict comes from understanding the role that brain functioning plays in this cycle. The second step requires using two strategies to examine past breakdowns and avoid them in the future. And the third step involves slowing down and quieting your emotional and physical responses to allow you to identify the situation not as an actual threat but as an uncomfortable experience that you can manage. In short, we can be trained to recognize and subvert our automatic, instinctual reactions so that we preserve a sense of control and intentional, thoughtful responding.

Neuroplasticity

According to Siegel (2010), "We can use our minds to change the activity and structure of the brain." With conscious awareness and focused attention, you can actually alter the way your neurons fire and change the linkages between them, which creates new circuitry in the brain. Pretty astounding, right? This process, called *neuroplasticity*, is particularly important for parents in high conflict. You hold the power to change your mind-set as it relates to your co-parent. And by changing your mind-set, you can redefine and transform your view and participation in the relationship and begin to get your children out of the "war zone." When you do this, they experience at least one parent who is at peace and is teaching them about resilience at the same time.

What we're saying is that you can use your mind to change your brain. By making a conscious decision that you are going to choose a life of peace for your children and create a neutral, business-like approach to parenting your children together, you (and perhaps your co-parent) can begin to change the conflict dynamic between you. You must refrain from taking the bait that hooks you into the conflict and causes you to justify your hostile behavior as a function of your co-parent's behavior. To better deal with conflict, it is important to practice and overlearn a response that overrides your fight, flight, or freeze response and protects you from amygdala hijack. Like the pilots in the earlier example, you must train yourself to have a "top-down" response, one that arises from your higher-level cortical functions—your thinking and rational brain— and put a protocol of "emergency preparedness" steps into action.

You can also recognize that there are things you don't know because you are human and have blind spots. If both parents take 100% responsibility for their own behavior in an interaction with the other and focus fully on themselves, there is less likelihood that you will automatically blame negative interactions on your co-parent.

Two Strategies to Break the Cycle of Conflict

Two valuable concepts to add to your vocabulary and skill set are what we call *20–20 hindsight* and what Daniel Siegel (2009) calls *mindsight*. These tools are extremely useful for looking back at breakdowns you've had with your co-parent and creating strategies to avoid them in the future. Often, a new level of understanding can be reached following a breakdown, one that allows for a different response that can change the conflict dynamic. In essence, we can turn "breakdowns" into "breakthroughs."

20–20 Hindsight

We are often able to look in the rearview mirror and see things that were not apparent to us during an emotionally charged and challenging moment. We call this 20–20 hindsight. This is particularly true for divorcing and divorced parents caught in a conflict dynamic. In the moment, it seems there is no other course of action than the one that is emotionally driven. With awareness and understanding that is drawn from 20–20 hindsight, though, you can prepare yourself for these inevitable moments the next time they occur. You can practice strategies to help you slow down, stop and think, or disengage so you're not overtaken by an amygdala hijack. Knowing how to stay in control and on the high road can help you detoxify the moment.

Mindsight

Daniel Siegel (2010) describes mindsight as a skill you can foster and develop that becomes a "transformational tool" you can use in your relationships. He sees this as something that can be developed in anyone, at any age, and despite any early history.

Mindsight is a kind of focused attention that allows us to see the internal workings of our own minds. It helps us to be aware of our mental processes without being swept away by them, enables us to get ourselves off the autopilot of ingrained behaviors and habitual responses, and moves us beyond the reactive emotional loops we all have a tendency to get trapped in. It lets us "name and tame" the emotions we are experiencing rather than being overwhelmed by them. (Siegel 2010)

Mindsight is a valuable tool for divorcing parents. By being able to focus a very sharp lens on your internal world, and in particular how you are interpreting and understanding yourself and your co-parenting partner, you can "resculpt your neural pathways, stimulating the growth of areas of the brain that are crucial to mental health" (Siegel 2010, loc. 135). This includes developing the capacity to reflect on your own behavior with openness, objectivity, and observation (Siegel 2010). When you have had a "low road moment," being able to look back on it with curiosity about your own triggers and your own process, rather than simply rehashing the events and justifying your reaction, is key. Look back at what happened; look inside and take responsibility for your words and actions. Committing yourself to develop and use these skills when you find yourself in the midst of conflict is a gift you can give to yourself and to your children.

Exercise 2.2: Using 20–20 Hindsight and Mindsight

Returning to your first journal entry in this chapter, look back at your description of an emotional reaction or outburst. Now look at that experience with 20–20 hindsight and mindsight. What might you have done to short-circuit that reaction? How could you have engaged your higher-level cortical functions— your thinking and reasoning brain—to change your response and influence the outcome? Write out your plan so you can come back to it in the future.

Slow Down and Focus on Your Breath

As you begin to develop 20–20 hindsight and mindsight, you can benefit from learning how to use your breath to help you through those moments you've identified as difficult moments. When you find yourself in a too-familiar moment of distress, you can slow yourself down and focus on your breath as a way of giving yourself time to formulate a thoughtful response. We will be discussing this in greater depth in chapter 3; however, let's take a moment and look at one way to slow down and focus on your breath.

Exercise 2.3: A Simple Breathing Exercise: Three-Part Breath

Sit or lie down in a quiet place and put one hand on your belly and the other on your heart. Begin to focus in on your breathing. Breathe in slowly and deeply through your nose. Notice your belly rising when you take a deep inhale, and feel the breath filling up your belly (part one), then your lungs (part two), and then your chest (part three). Pause for a moment and breathe out slowly through your mouth, and feel the warm breath leaving your chest, lungs, and belly. Notice how the breath is cool when it enters your nostrils, and warm when you breathe out through your mouth. Take ten deep breaths, using your awareness of your three-part breath. Note whether and how you feel differently after the ten breaths. What changed? Do you have any greater sense of comfort after doing this exercise? You can use this and other methods of focusing on your breath whenever you are stressed or need to center yourself. Your breath is always with you, a tool you can leverage to calm yourself and stay solidly in your centered self.

Turning Crisis into Opportunity

In postdivorce parenting relationships, breakdowns are inevitable. In fact, there are certain times of change during which they are often predictable. Recognizing the conditions that may set the stage for a breakdown can help you understand the source of your own emotional response and help you become prepared for those moments. It also can help you accept responsibility for your "low road" behaviors with self-compassion (not shame), and thus help you recover more quickly. Going back to the example of Cara and Zach, the backdrop for the breakdown was the distress over the dog's serious illness and everything surrounding that event. Moves and life-cycle rituals like graduations, confirmations, baptisms, births, and deaths can be triggering times. Certainly, when one of you remarries or makes a commitment to a new significant other, or has another child, the conditions for breakdowns are set in motion.

But you can take the high road. You can seek professional help to be prepared for the increased stress and tension during these times if you need extra support in developing your preparedness strategies. You can apply your new understanding of how the brain functions and the potential for finding yourself overtaken by your monkey brain and primed to retaliate; in this way you can be "armed and prepared" to counter these reactions with strategies to engage your higher cortical functions and be faster to move to repair ruptures. In fact, awareness in these moments can create opportunities for breakthroughs in understanding and more long-term stability in your co-parenting relationship.

Exercise 2.4: Turning Crisis into Opportunity

Look back at a time in your co-parenting relationship when every interaction felt brittle and likely to explode. In your journal, describe what was happening at the time. You may see patterns here. Contrast this with periods of greater trust and flexibility as co-parents. What conditions or events triggered the breakdowns? What conditions or events triggered healthier co-parenting interactions? Can you see a way that you could have turned (or did turn) the crisis into an opportunity? What might help create more success in a similar situation?

You can be the parent who begins to make constructive changes. Don't wait for the other parent to go first. Transforming your high-conflict parenting relationship to one of neutrality, or even reaching a place where you can honor the bond you have with your co-parent, can create enormous opportunities—including teaching your children about resilience in relationships. You can take the lead.

Wrapping It Up

In this chapter we introduced the science of interpersonal neurobiology and described the functioning of your three-part brain. When you are in chronic conflict, the amygdala can hijack your higher-level brain functioning, making it is easy to flip your lid and take the low road. To counter this tendency and prepare yourself to handle the inevitable breakdowns that can occur with your co-parent, you can use the valuable tools of 20–20 hindsight and mindsight. In our next chapter, we will discuss ways to manage your emotional responses, addressing concepts of shame, dignity, and mindfulness, and learning emotion regulation strategies.

Taking It Home and Making It Yours

* Develop an awareness of what triggers or provokes you into "flipping your lid," and anticipate those moments. Create your own strategy to use when you are faced with that provocation.

* Create a pledge to yourself that for your children's sake, especially when they are watching, you will not allow yourself to get hooked into amygdala hijacks.

❋ Practice and overlearn your strategies to handle stressful inter-actions, like the pilots we discussed in this chapter. Emergency preparedness training is key.

❋ Use your 20–20 hindsight to analyze breakdowns and create breakthroughs. Look back at situations that imploded or exploded and try to see them in slow motion. Create a strategy for how you will handle these in the future.

❋ Practice developing your mindsight by being able to "name and tame" your emotions. Focus a sharp lens on your reactions to identify the triggers, and be vigilant when you see them coming so you can respond to them in a calm, neutral way as if it had nothing to do with you.

❋ Practice simple breathing techniques such as the three-part breath and other self-soothing strategies.

CHAPTER 3

Skills and Strategies for Emotion Regulation

Your emotions do, as you saw in chapter 2, have an impact on your *brain*, which then of course has an impact on your *body*. However, there is a third part of our being to consider: the *mind*. The mind is made up of our conscious thoughts and perceptions (those that we are aware of) as well as our unconscious thoughts and perceptions (those that we are not aware of). Both our conscious and unconscious thoughts and perceptions impact our bodies, behavior, and reactions to others. Your emotions, your body, and your mind all influence one another. In this chapter, we introduce the concept of emotion regulation, which is the ability to change your thoughts and perceptions in order to respond differently to a situation that you cannot change. We also address new concepts of your inherent worth, compassionate witness, mindfulness, and affirmations.

The Mind's Effect on Our Experience

Take a simple example of three strangers, Amy, Bill, and Carly, seeing the same movie in the same theater at the same time. They happen to be sitting next to one another in the same row. The movie is a love story wrapped up in a spy thriller plot. After the movie ends, they text the following to their friends:

Amy: What a wonderful and exciting love story!

Bill: The movie was a sappy love story but a great
          thriller mystery.

Carly: It was gory, stupid, and unbelievable at times.
          Don't bother.

What happened here? Amy, Bill, and Carly had three different reactions to the same exact stimulus (the movie). In fact, we might argue that their reactions were not even to something real, but were based on the manufactured images and sounds that were present in the film. What accounted for the three different reactions?

If you said, "what they each brought to the movie," or "who they are," or something similar, you'd be right. All three moviegoers walked into the theater with their own history and experiences and ways of viewing things—their own baggage. This then led to different experiences to the same event.

If you then asked them what they were feeling, you might hear the following:

Amy: I feel great. What a terrific experience!

Bill: That was exciting, even though the love story was
          little over the top.

Carly: What a waste of my time and money. I'm disappointed.

What they each said to themselves influenced their reactions. The movie didn't do anything to them. It didn't independently *make* them feel a certain way. How they reacted to it was based on who they each are and the sum of their prior experiences. Amy, Bill, and Carly were not the same when they came into the movie, and they were not the same when they left.

While life is not a movie, we (and others, including your co-parent) often place a lot more emphasis on what the other did to us than on how we interpreted it and how we responded. In a failing or failed marriage, this process is all too familiar. You see the things your spouse has done that have hurt, frustrated, and disappointed you. You expected one thing from the marriage and have gotten something else. In many cases, the same is true for your co-parent. He came to the marriage with his own experience and way of looking at love, intimacy, and companionship. As the marriage failed, he probably became quite verbal (perhaps enraged) and told you the ways you failed him. He may have repeatedly told you these things throughout the course of the marriage, in essence telling you how the script he expected to see on the screen (or how he wanted you to be) was not being acted out. Let's look at how this may have played out in your marriage.

Exercise 3.1: My Co-parent's Script

In your journal, write down the three most disturbing things your co-parent has blamed you for. In other words, write down hurtful examples of when you heard remarks like "It's your fault I'm upset. If you hadn't _____, everything would be okay."

This is your co-parent's script. Just as we learned in the movie theater scenario, the script is likely based on your co-parent's early experiences and how those impacted his functioning in the relationship and his expectations of you both during and after the marriage. You cannot change this script, as it does not belong to you. It belongs to your co-parent. It would be like trying to convince Carly that she should reevaluate and enjoy the movie. Her impression, her opinions, and what she was looking for from the movie are hers and unlikely to change, no matter how much logic or persuasion you try to use.

Next, write down your usual responses to these criticisms. How much energy did you, and do you still, spend trying to change your co-parent's impressions and reactions to you? Did you try to meet the mountain of his expectations, only to find upon reaching the top that there was another mountain to climb? What are your reactions to his complaints and disappointment? Do you react with withdrawal (flight), saying,

"That's it. He is impossible. I'm done. I'm just not going to respond"? Or do you react with counterblame or justification (fight), saying, "You're blaming me for that? How can you say that? Look at how *you've* been. You can't even take responsibility for what you do and how you mess things up!"? Of course, you might just go blank until the storm passes (freeze) and find you just can't say anything in response.

Your reaction is yours, not a reflex to the actions of your co-parent.

Changing Your Perspective

You can learn to respond differently. This means looking at the way your own mind works. You are in essence watching your co-parent's movie, as your co-parent is watching yours. That is, you are reacting to him with all that you bring to the relationship.

You may find that you cannot get out of the bind of asking yourself, in response to his being upset about your behavior, *Why does [name] keep treating me like this after all this time, when all I try to do is the right thing?* This loop can repeat endlessly because it does not lead to a change in your perspective, or his. Instead, it is important to start asking yourself questions such as *Why do I keep expecting my co-parent to "get it"? Why do I expect him to see my efforts? Why do I keep reacting to his anger as I do?*

The next exercise may help you begin to change your perspective.

Exercise 3.2: The Tirade

Imagine that your co-parent attacks your character after you have been late getting the children ready for the transition to their other home, or some other event that occurs regularly in your experience with your co-parent. Imagine yourself in the midst of your co-parent's tirade. Don't defend yourself from the attack. In fact, what happens if instead of looking at it as an attack, you simply look at the comments as those of someone who is upset (regardless of whom they are upset with). Write down in your journal how you would respond if it *wasn't* about you. What if *your best friend* or *next door neighbor* was telling you this story? You would listen but not take it personally. Pay attention to the difference in your own feelings from this perspective. When you listen to the story from your friend or neighbor, you don't question your self worth. Her emotional response is completely unrelated to your worth. Why should this change if the person telling the story is your co parent? We don't believe it should.

In a sense, you are the movie your co-parent is evaluating. Her reactions are *hers*. While she claims it is about you, it really is about her, or what she brought to or wanted from the relationship. It may even be about what she still wants from the relationship—how she wants you to be now. Your co-parent's disapproval is not really about you, but about how you are not living up to *her expectations* of you. If you say to yourself, *I must live up to her expectations of me*, then you become trapped into feeling the emotional distress due to taking responsibility for someone else's experience. It is as if Amy feels guilty because Carly hated the movie. Even if they knew each other and Amy picked the movie, Carly's reaction is not Amy's doing. Amy did not cause the reaction. Did this exercise help you see that your co-parent's actions do not *cause* your reactions?

Your Mind and the Stories You Tell Yourself

We've been looking at what your former spouse says about you. Now let's make it a bit more difficult. Let's look at how the process also works in the other direction—what you say about your co-parent. This is where your emotions can really get revved up.

Exercise 3.3: My Blame List

In your journal, make a table with three columns labeled as follows:

I blame my co-parent for...

How I feel about it

My contributions to the situation

What are the three most disturbing things you blame your co-parent for? Write these in the first column. In the second column, write how they have made you feel. Now the hard part; take some time with this. Try to be as honest as you can, speaking from the voice in your mind that interprets your experience and feels hurt and upset, and write in the third column what you are bringing to these three situations. What are you telling yourself about how awful or terrible these things are and their overall impact on you? What are you saying should be, or should have been? How should your co-parent have acted? Notice the intensity of what you said.

Here is where you have the chance to begin to get some control. It is not about what happened, but how you look at what happened and the significance you give it. Let's look at some elements of your "story," or as some professionals call it, your narrative. If you said the three things you or your partner did were "awful," "terrible," "catastrophic," or something similar, you are on your way to feeling depressed, victimized, and out of control. These words define the magnitude of the problem, but they are, in many ways, rather subjective.

While your divorce may feel like an awful experience, if you try to look at it objectively, you might be able to recognize that there may be other events or situations that could be far worse. That does not make your divorce less painful; it just can put it in a different perspective. Let's take a moment to look at the divorce from a more overarching perspective.

Is there truly nothing worse than your marriage falling apart, or even the way it fell apart? Where does this fall on the scale of all the terrible things that could befall someone? Of course, the end of the marriage is not typically a happy or wonderful experience, even if you initiated the divorce, but is it the worst experience a human being could have? On a 10-point scale of awful events, with 10 being the worst experience possible and 0 being not bad at all, where does the divorce rank? It is certainly not a 0, and in all likelihood it is quite a bit above a 5. However, is it a 10? Keeping it in perspective can help change what your brain and emotions do with this stressor.

If you view the divorce as a major, longstanding stressor, your body will react differently than if you view it as equivalent to a stress of epic proportions: getting diagnosed with a life-threatening disease, being a victim of a terrorist attack, being hit by a tsunami, and so on. Imagine if you shifted the perspective or the narrative. Your body and emotions respond to how you view the situation—the movie of your own life.

The Role of Shame

Researcher Brené Brown has studied the emotion of shame extensively. She describes shame as being a universal emotion that emanates from our wish and need to be perfect and fit in (Brown 2012). When we are feeling judged or ridiculed about some aspect of ourselves (our looks, work, parenting, family, spending habits, choice of spouse, or role in our marriage), we feel shame. We also judge ourselves harshly, leading to self-inflicted shame. We experience shame when we are not feeling worthy and accepted by ourselves and others.

When you've experienced a breakdown with your co-parent and one or both of you have engaged in the fight, flight, or freeze response, the ruptures in your relationship that already exist are deepened. Often following such incidents you are likely to feel shame, embarrassment, and a sense of remorse or regret. You may think, *How could I have let her get to me like that?* You may also feel embarrassed that others witnessed your response and wonder, *What is wrong with me?* or *How could I have behaved like that? That's not me.* Knowing others have witnessed your reaction, you may feel even more ashamed or humiliated. You can think of it as a formula:

Reactivity = Shame

It is particularly difficult to try to repair a breach or rupture in the relationship when you are feeling a sense of shame and vulnerability, particularly with someone you no longer trust. By understanding how the brain works and how the high-conflict interaction sets you up for a chronic state of high alert, you can recognize an encounter that ended with an amygdala hijack (chapter 2). As you realize that your brain was activated in a way that became out of your control for a time, you can let go of self-blame and shame and move toward compassion for your own humanity as well as for the humanity of your co-parent. You also can focus on using this awareness to gain more control in future situations that evoke the same emotional reaction.

When you have taken the low road, it is critical to follow up with a repair, even if it is an acknowledgment that you did not respond well. A simple, "I'm sorry for the way I reacted and what I said" can go a long way to helping you push the reset button. When you take accountability and responsibility, you are operating with integrity, authenticity, presence, and strength to make a repair to this critical parenting relationship that is at the heart of your children's emotional safety and stability.

In this next exercise, you will have a chance to look back at your own feelings of shame following a moment in which you flipped your lid.

Exercise 3.4: My Shame

Returning to the three critical moments you described in the previous exercise, look at each one carefully and think about whether you felt shame after your response. Rate your sense of shame on a scale of 0 to 10, with 10 being something you're deeply ashamed of, and 0 being no awareness of feeling shame. If you find that your sense of shame is on the high end of the scale, can you recognize your own humanity and value, and forgive yourself for losing your footing in that situation? Plan your strategy for reacting with clarity and calm the next time you are so provoked. What do you need to do differently? Please write it down in your journal.

The Role of Dignity

Researcher Donna Hicks (2011) has written extensively about the role of dignity in resolving conflict. The concept of dignity underscores your inherent worth and value as a human being. Think of the perfection of a newborn baby and the inherent value of that baby. Your dignity—your inherent value as a human being—cannot be taken away from you. It is yours at birth, as your birthright, and yours throughout your life. From early on and throughout your life, you are subject to violations of dignity in the form of psychological hurts or injuries at the hands of another, some of which are inflicted purposely, others unintentionally. Research has shown that psychological injuries activate the same area of the brain that registers physical pain. While we acknowledge and treat physical injuries immediately, we are not as quick to acknowledge violations to our dignity, which can lead to shame, humiliation, or damage to our sense of self-worth. In the example we read in chapter 2, when Cara and Zach found themselves hijacked by their emotions and taken over by their fight instincts, both inflicted dignity violations upon the other. Both felt justified in saying horrible and hurtful things to each other.

In many highly conflictual co-parenting interactions, the threat is not usually to physical survival; it is to your dignity. Parents in high conflict trigger these survival reactions in each other. When you are caught in the grip of ongoing dignity violations and escalating conflict, your monkey-brain reactions leave you completely unprepared and unable to access your higher-level thinking and problem-solving capacities. As a result, you injure one another repeatedly and come to your interactions primed and armed for conflict—"a fight waiting to happen."

Let's analyze the interaction between Zach and Cara in the prior chapter. Both were in a vulnerable place to begin with. The wounds resulting from the relationship breakdown and betrayal that preceded their divorce were still raw. Both had inflicted multiple dignity violations on the other. Add to this the high emotion of a triggering event like deciding how to best deal with the serious illness of the family pet. Even before this development, Cara was easily triggered by a word or phrase that Zach uttered. He had repeatedly violated her dignity during the marriage, and at the time the marriage crumbled, her psychological injuries were compounded exponentially. When triggered, she would eviscerate Zach with her harsh words and character judgment, laying all the blame for the failure of their marriage and emotional pain of their children at his feet. Her direct attacks on Zach's character violated his dignity—his basic sense of value and self-worth. Provoked and activated, all thought of the impact on their children and their ultimate goals went out the window. Zach then would attack back in the harshest way he could, blaming the disintegration of the marriage completely on Cara, and violating her dignity once more. Once they were in this place, their brains were awash in the neurotransmitters that stand at the ready to respond to threats to their survival. Their capacity to use their higher-level brain functions was short-circuited.

Following this breakdown, both Cara and Zach were experiencing a sense of shame as well as continued justification for their belief that the other parent was impossible to deal with, putting them and their children at risk of psychological harm. Both were unable to acknowledge the pain they had inflicted on the other, and neither saw the need for repair with the other. As a result, they moved forward primed for more and more breakdowns, which would leave their children feeling unsafe and vulnerable, having two parents who are living in a war zone, caught in a self-perpetuating cycle of conflict, ready to melt down at any given moment.

Exercise 3.5: Identifying Violations of My Dignity

Return to exercise 3.2, and look again at your response to your co-parent's imagined attack on you. List the violations of your dignity that occurred during this attack. Can you identify the violations of your co-parent's dignity? Did you find yourself retaliating with a dignity violation when you experienced one?

Now list the steps you can take to hold on to your own dignity, whatever violations your co-parent may make. Think about your answers to the following questions, and write them down in your journal: How can you be certain of your own worth, regardless of your co-parent's opinions? How can you refrain from violating the dignity of your co-parent, even if he or she has violated yours? How can you commit to being the one to stop the cycle?

When you feel that your dignity has been violated in an interaction with your parenting partner, you are responsible for speaking up and addressing the violation. However, an important point here is to figure out *whom* we need to speak up to when our dignity is violated. Most people speak up to their co-parent, as if the co-parent is the one who is causing the dignity violation. However, another way of looking at this is to recognize that your dignity and worth are inherent from the moment you are born. They are not based on the comments of the audience who is in front of you at the moment. In essence, you inadvertently give away your dignity when you allow the comments of your co-parent to get to you. Of course, when this happens you feel attacked and then feel the need to defend your own sense of self against the onslaught.

However, imagine if you completely and firmly knew that your worth was not dependent on the comments of your co-parent. That is, imagine if you knew in your heart that your co-parent's comments about you (whether good or bad) did not for one moment change the solid, inherent worth that has and will always be there. Your co-parent can tell you that you are the best or the worst person or parent in the world, but that won't change the truth of the person and parent you are. If you are certain about your own worth, the attacks of the other don't really matter. You also don't have to chase after appreciation and compliments to get a more solid sense of self. Those don't define you either. Understanding your own contribution to the problem—your own reaction to what your co-parent said or did—can help you gain control and avoid feeling victimized by the complaints and criticism that come your way.

The Role of Compassion

You may find it relatively easy to be compassionate to someone you care about. You can offer care, support, and at times optimism (without false hope). You even can help the person gain insight. Yet this is far more difficult when it comes to looking at yourself.

If you grew up in an environment that was demanding, harsh, or critical, it would have been easy to incorporate this negative language into your own view of yourself (without even realizing it). Your heart might be open and supportive to others, yet there might be a different standard when it comes to yourself. You'd be the exception to your own rule of offering kindness and compassion when you witness someone's pain. When you witness your own pain (even about things besides your divorce), a critical and even scolding and demeaning voice may come to mind. This voice then activates the emotional and physical responses we spoke about in earlier chapters. It is as if you are your own threat—a threat to your very sense of self.

Being a Compassionate Witness

Most of us find it easier to be compassionate to someone other than ourselves. It may be easy for you not to judge someone else harshly, yet you turn around and judge yourself with a much tougher set of standards. Imagine if you taught yourself to be as compassionate to yourself as you are to someone else—to be a *compassionate witness*. It is like modifying the golden rule to say, "Treat yourself as compassionately as you treat someone else." Elizabeth Lesser (2008) writes about this in her book *Broken Open* as she tells the story of her own marital crisis and the lessons she learned along her way to recovery. With practice, you can learn to be your own compassionate witness, an important step on your own journey of recovery.

Exercise 3.6: My Compassionate Witness

Now, return to your answers in exercise 3.1, My Co-parent's Script, and respond to them as if a dear, loving friend had said that about his or her life. What would you say? How would you show compassion to your friend around each of the three items listed? Speak from your heart. Do not offer false assurances and pity. Offer loving friendship. Write down these loving responses.

What did you feel as you were adopting a more compassionate (not victimized or self-incriminating) perspective to yourself? Did it shift the focus from what happened to you, or what you did or did not do, to healing and moving forward? A compassionate response is about nurturance, not blame. It does not deny that there is a problem or challenge, but recognizes what can come from that challenge. When you direct your compassion to yourself, you can avoid the harsh, scolding parental voice you may hear in your mind. Instead you can soothe your emotions and react with a calming, loving (and yes, at the same time realistic) voice. That is the voice of a healthy parent or a good friend who is truly there for you. And yes, it can be your own voice.

Turning Self-Blame into Self-Compassion

We've talked about how to take the focus off of how you've been blamed by your co-parent, and perhaps others; now let's turn to an even more difficult topic: what you blame yourself for. Some of the most upsetting things are not those that the other person says about us but rather what we say about ourselves. It is bad enough to hear from your former spouse, sometimes over and over, a litany of things that you did wrong. However, how many times have you blamed yourself? While your former spouse is not always present to blame you, you are always there to blame yourself—thousands of times.

The problem with blaming yourself is that it hurts the very core of who you are. It hurts your self-esteem and ignores your positive traits. We are not saying that you should disregard your role in the marriage and its falling part. Rather, we are telling you not to blame yourself in a hurtful or cruel way.

These next two exercises are about self-blame. Please take your time with these journal entries. You may find them difficult.

Exercise 3.7: My Self-Blame List

Write about your role in the problems or ending of the marriage. What did you do or not do that led to problems? Do not list your co-parent's complaints of you. Rather, list what you in your heart know to be true. Perhaps your former spouse does not even know about the things you write. Perhaps they are secrets that only you know. You can even write them in "code" if you are afraid someone will find your journal. Pay attention to the feelings you experience. Sit with these feelings. Do not rush. Do not run from the pain. Then, list the feelings that are the strongest. Now, put the journal aside for a few moments. Allow yourself some time to recover, if needed, and then come back to pick up where you left off.

Next, we are going to ask you to take on the demeanor of a close friend or relative—a compassionate witness—as you consider ways you have blamed yourself.

Exercise 3.8: Returning to Compassion

This time, write a compassionate, caring, honest response. What would you say to a sibling, adult child, or dear friend who opened up and shared with you the pain and perhaps guilt in what you just read in your self-blame list in exercise 3.7? Write those compassionate responses in this journal entry. Notice the differences in how you feel when you view the reality of what happened compassionately instead of critically. What happens to your level of emotional pain? What happens to your tension? What happens deep within your heart?

The mind plays tricks on us. It tells us rational and irrational things. Our emotions and our body react to what the mind perceives both consciously and unconsciously. Often we behave based on these perceptions and thoughts, even if they are not in our best interests and cause us incredible amounts of pain. Yet, when we instruct our mind to focus as a compassionate witness (the lens we would use with someone we care about) on ourselves, we can have a different and caring perspective—even when we are displeased with the very actions we have taken.

Calming the Mind with Compassion

Just as we can calm a friend, a child, and even a baby, we can calm ourselves. While often it is with words, it does not have to be. A baby does not have language and yet can be calmed by a stranger, if that person's heart is open and the baby feels a sense of safety and love. Unfortunately, in divorce, many people have experienced their former partner's, or their own, closed heart as the marriage fractured and dissolved. This closing of the heart makes compassion difficult, even for yourself. Compassion for yourself may have been difficult even before you were married. (Remember the baggage that our viewers took to the movie?) Many people have learned self-degradation and neglect from childhood. They have learned that self-care and responding to one's needs is "selfish" and "narcissistic." It's not. When people who are selfish or narcissistic respond to their own needs, it is usually accompanied by a complete disregard for the other person. Being compassionate toward oneself does not necessarily exclude the other person. It just does not exclude yourself. Caring for your self and being selfish are two different things.

Let's take a few moments to look at this using a few journal entries.

Exercise 3.9: Increasing Compassion

As you think about your divorce...

A. Write and complete the sentence: "It is impossible to..."

B. Now change the word *impossible* to *difficult* and rewrite the full sentence. What do you notice?

C. Now, be the compassionate friend that you can be to someone you care deeply for and respond to the first prompt (It is impossible to...). Write that response in your journal. What differences do you notice in the third response compared with the first? Which would you rather hear from a compassionate friend? Is one truth and the other fiction? Or, is it not about "truth" but rather about which way you view the "movie" of your experience?

Let's try another statement. Thinking about your divorce...

A. Write and complete the sentence: It is awful that...

B. Now change the word *awful* to *stressful* and rewrite the full sentence. What do you notice?

C. Now, be the compassionate friend that you can be to someone you care deeply for and respond to the first prompt. Here again, be very attentive to what you notice as you change the script. How do the answers lead to different feelings and even physical sensations?

Let's try one more statement about your divorce...

A. Write and complete the sentence: I was so stupid to...

B. Now change *I was so stupid to* to *I wish I hadn't* and rewrite the full sentence. What do you notice?

C. Now, be the compassionate friend that you can be to someone you care deeply for and respond to the first prompt.

Notice the difference as you move from sentence A to sentence B to sentence C. Did you notice a difference in your calmness? While we cannot always change what happens to us (like getting soaked in an unexpected summer rainstorm), we can change how we view it. We can be the person who says, "Ugh, my day is ruined! Look at me; I'm soaking wet down to my socks. What bad luck I have on the one day I was so stupid to forget my umbrella." Alternatively, we can be the person who says, "Wow. What a storm! Good thing I don't melt." It is the same life movie. Different views. Different feelings. Which view, which narrative, works better for you? Your control is in deciding what story you tell yourself, rather than defining yourself by what other people (for example your co-parent) tell you who have viewed you as their "movie."

———————————————————————

Next, we are going to ask you to look at three upsetting co-parenting situations that may provide a more difficult challenge.

Exercise 3.10: My Hot-Button Situations

In your journal, create a table with three columns:

Three situations in which my co-parent upsets me

What I say to myself in this situation

What my compassionate friend would say to me

In the first column, list three common situations in which your co-parent really upsets you. These may be related to petty issues blown out of proportion, long-standing gripes about you, or situations that are intense, unpleasant, and perhaps scary. Here again, describe each situation in detail. In the second column, jot down what you said to yourself in each situation. And in the third column, offer yourself a compassionate response, as if you were speaking to a friend. You can even offer advice to this friend. How would you suggest to your friend that she react to her co-parent's complaints and behaviors? Should she internalize them? Should she believe the criticism? Should she try to just say or do the "magic" thing (as if there was one) that will change her former partner's opinion of herself?

Can you offer a response that recognizes your friend's value, goodness, and worth and perhaps helps avoid perpetuating conflict that has no end point? In fact, what if you assumed that her co-parent would always be as upset? What if you looked at her co-parent as the movie your friend is watching? It will always be the same movie. How would you suggest she respond to reduce her emotional reactivity and distress? How would you suggest she key into her own worth and goodness? How would you offer compassion, love, and kindness to your friend?

Work slowly on this. Go back and edit your responses until you have them just right.

Emotion Regulation Strategies

Emotion regulation is not about changing the world around you (in this case the comments and behaviors of your former partner); it is about changing your own responses to the world as it is. This is not a new concept. For hundreds, if not thousands, of years, people across many cultures have had to deal with crises, traumas, and catastrophes of all sorts. They have focused on changing their perceptions and thoughts when they couldn't change the situation. They have learned compassion to self and others as a way of providing caring and healthy reassurance. Many cultures also have focused on what is often termed *quieting the mind* as a way of soothing oneself, staying calm, and dealing with stress.

Quieting the Mind

There are references to the benefits of such strategies in various spiritual and religious practices, the martial arts, high-intensity athletics, and many of the performing arts. You have probably heard of terms such as *meditation, mindfulness, self-hypnosis, relaxation training, biofeedback,* and even Lamaze techniques for childbirth. All of these are descriptions of different approaches to get to the point of a quieter mind. Religious experts have even described prayer as such a pathway.

Often our mind is like a car radio scanning many stations. This is particularly evident late at night if you cannot sleep. Your mind probably jumps from station to station as you think about all sorts of things—the tasks on your to-do list, what happened with your children today, what your lawyer said, why your co-parent took a particular position on an issue, why all of this is happening to you and seems like it will never end, and on and on. You probably find yourself even circling back to the same thoughts over and over, as the mind acts like a person lost in the woods, going back over the same ground, seeing the same trees and not finding the way out. To make matters worse, this leads to more tension and wakefulness, making it even more difficult to fall asleep.

You're not alone, and no, you're not crazy. Your mind is revved up and needs to quiet down. Since ancient times, cultures have studied quieting the mind. Some very simple concepts have emerged and have withstood the test of time. We have gleaned these concepts from our studies and the writings of authors from many different fields, such as Buddhism and other spiritual and religious practices, mental health concepts and treatment approaches, and performance enhancement. Although it may be easy to reject them as overly simplistic and therefore not beneficial, when practiced they can indeed be quite helpful at bringing a sense of calmness and even clarity in thinking and problem solving.

Let's briefly look at some of the key elements of these practices and how they relate to high-conflict divorce. Feel free to stop at any point and experiment with these meditations and other practices. See what you notice, what you feel, and what you hear as you listen to your mind, and perhaps more importantly your heart. Feel free to write your experiences in your journal.

Applying Focus

Instead of switching quickly back and forth between the radio stations of the mind, the practice of focusing has you limit the (at times frantic) shifting back and forth of the mind. This is done by teaching your mind to concentrate on your breathing and to let your thoughts pass by without dwelling on them. Rather than thinking, it is about just *being*. You actually move beyond your thoughts and are far more "in the moment," present with whatever you are feeling or doing at the time. If you are meditating, the focus may simply be on the experience of meditating. If you are exercising, the focus may be just on the experience of exercising. Many times coaches, gurus, yoga instructors, and therapists will suggest that you focus on your breathing, slowing your breathing to a rhythmic pattern. This does not have to be done as a formal meditation over a long period of time and in some formal (and perhaps uncomfortable) position. Rather, you can just sit comfortably, perhaps with quiet music, incense, or a candle (if you find it helpful), and allow yourself to not think about all the problems of the day. Notice we said, "allow yourself," not "try." When we try, we tense. Quieting is about not tensing. It is about allowing yourself to go to a more basic place and allowing your body and mind to "be," just as it is—even if it is tense, and even if you are thinking about your divorce. Yes, even if you are angry, depressed, overwhelmed, or anxious, you can just be. For babies, this comes naturally. They just are, in the moment, as they are, until the next set of moments.

Exercise 3.11: Just Being

So, even if it feels silly, strange, or uncomfortable, take a few minutes and just sit quietly. If your mind wanders, just notice it (try not to judge it, or yourself). Let your thoughts come and go, and gently refocus on your breathing, on a pleasant image, or on nothing.

Think about what you noticed. What did you feel? Did the time fly by or seem to drag? Did you think about the stress of the divorce? Did your mind wander or stay focused? There are no right or wrong answers here. It is just about giving yourself the opportunity to sit and experiment with quieting your mind. If you decide to allow yourself this opportunity on a regular basis, you may notice some important changes in your experience.

This meditative experience can be complicated by an active mind. You may find that your mind's radio stations seem to be out of your control—playing, as if it were 2 a.m. and you wanted to sleep. You might even find that there are intrusive thoughts. Even the hostile words of your former partner may come into your consciousness as you find yourself thinking, *Even here? I'm trying to relax and you follow me here? I can't believe it. This is impossible.*

No, it isn't impossible. This is a normal reaction to all you've been through. It is not at all uncommon for the intrusive and painful thoughts to emerge as you quiet down and give yourself the opportunity to take more control over your thoughts and consciousness. However, you do not have to be a victim to these thoughts or this process.

In the last exercise, did you find yourself saying, *I better not think about this*, or *I shouldn't be thinking about this*? Just like dieting can cause us to think more about food, telling ourselves not to think about something can cause us to think about it more because the words associated with the thoughts are triggers for more thoughts.

Exercise 3.12: Allowing My Thoughts

This time, try a different approach. When the thoughts come, breathe deeply and allow them. That's right. Don't fight them. Just notice them and allow them. Then, when you're ready, shift to something neutral or positive. Kindly say to yourself that you are going to shift (even briefly) to something else.

Notice the lack of judgment in just allowing the thoughts to be there. Compare this with the thoughts you had during the previous exercise, most likely full of shoulds and should nots and possibly ending with a statement of hopelessness (*This is impossible*). Sometimes, these statements can even be criticisms of ourselves (technically called *negative attributions*), which then get us even more upset and distracted. Experiment with being as supportive to yourself as you would be toward someone you care for. Giving yourself the same support as you would to a loved one can give you a sense of relief and empowerment.

Mindfulness

Living in the moment is the essence of *mindfulness*, commonly defined as a "state of active, open, intentional attention on the present." Being aware of your thoughts moment to moment as an observer or witness rather than a judge allows you to wake up to your experience as opposed to letting your life go by without actually living it. Particularly in this age of electronic devices, screens, and distractions, it is so easy not to be present in the present, and to spend our time interacting with a virtual world, worrying about the future or ruminating about the past. Jon Kabat-Zinn (1990) defines mindfulness as "paying attention in a particular way: on purpose, in the present moment and nonjudgmentally." You can practice mindfulness in everyday activities as routine as eating, driving, cooking, walking your dog, or washing the dishes. You can do this by actively focusing your attention only on what you're doing in the moment. For example, when you're eating, pay attention to your food: How does it look, smell, taste? What is the texture of it? How does it feel in your mouth? Chew slowly and enjoy the sensations. Are you getting satiated as you eat? When you're driving, pay attention to steering the car, staying in your lane, the other cars around you, road conditions, and so on. When you're walking your dog, stay present with the experience of being outdoors with your pet—the sensations, sights, and sounds of nature around you. Pay attention to your dog's movements and activity, your own breath, your heart rate, and the feeling of your joints and muscles as you move through space.

Why is mindfulness important for co-parents in conflict? The short answer: It's all about the children. They deserve nothing less. It is all too easy for parents in conflict to lose sight of the moment-to-moment experience of their children. The strong emotions that accompany high-conflict divorce and postdivorce life (described in chapters 1 and 2) can leave even the best parents vulnerable to losing their focus on the present moment and how their interactions appear when looking through the eyes of their children.

Consider this scenario. Doug and Beth are in the throes of a very painful divorce, and Beth feels deeply betrayed and humiliated in their community. Doug understands the hurt that he has caused and is conscious of how fragile things are between Beth and himself in this moment. Beth is trying hard to put the needs of the children front and center, so when Doug calls her home at dinnertime, with all four children seated at the table, she picks up and interrupts their dinner for all the children to speak with their dad. Things quickly deteriorate in the conversation, as Doug talks about plans he has made for the children, and their eldest child indicates that he doesn't want to participate. Doug gets upset and says a few choice words to his son on speakerphone, implying that Beth is to blame, and she then gets involved, loses her perspective, and begins expressing her anger and hurt about the divorce and how Doug is behaving toward the children. The children have a front-row seat. Their dinner is spoiled, everyone is upset, and now chaos reigns at Beth's home. The moment will pass, but the memories will be long lasting for the children.

Looking at this moment from a mindful perspective, if Beth had been paying attention, on purpose, to the experience of having dinner with her children, she might have allowed the phone call to go to her answering machine and preserved a peaceful family dinner, calling Doug back when they had finished. Even if she had answered the call, Doug, recognizing that the children were all sitting down to dinner with their mom, would have suggested he call back when they are finished and would have chosen not to have a conversation over speakerphone raising touchy topics, but rather speak separately with each child when they were done and free to speak.

Parents who remain in conflict postdivorce and expose their children to it repeatedly can leave their children's memories of childhood contaminated, and perhaps even poisoned, as discussed in our introduction. These are the childhood memories that the children will carry with them into adulthood. Baseball games, school plays and concerts, bar and bat mitzvahs, confirmations, graduations, birthday parties, and the lasting memories of them can be ruined unless you and your co-parent actively work to become mindful of your own and your children's day-to-day experience. By doing so, you can plan to manage and contain situations that have the potential to lead to conflict.

Developing Awareness of Three States of Mind

One of the fundamental skills you can develop is becoming aware of and being able to label your state of mind at any given moment, particularly when you are anticipating or engaged in an interaction with your co-parent that threatens to escalate into conflict. When you begin to understand and identify which of the three states of mind you are in, you can know when you are in the "right" state of mind to respond to your co-parent in a way that will quiet conflict rather than fan the flames. The first step is becoming aware of the different mind states, the second step is being able to identify when your mind is in each of these states, and the third is disengaging when you are in a state of mind where you are likely to end up in conflict.

Earlier we mentioned the DBT approach, founded by Marsha Linehan. One of the skills that DBT offers to individuals in distress is the understanding of the three different states of mind, which Linehan (1993) calls "emotion mind," "reasonable mind," and "wise mind." She also offers a way to observe and witness our own mind-state at any given time. To help parents relate to these states of mind, we have defined these concepts as extending beyond the mind to the *self*, and we are referring to them as *monkey-brain self*, *facts-and-logic self*, and *centered self*. For parents in chronic conflict, becoming conscious of your own state of mind and your unique emotional triggers offers you an opportunity to train yourself to check your emotional response when you're provoked and avoid being hijacked by your co-parent's (or your own) monkey-brain self, which can potentially lead to flipping your lid and engaging in chronic cycles of conflict.

Monkey-brain self. You experience your monkey-brain self as "hot," compared with your facts-and-logic self, which feels "cool." When you are in your monkey-brain self, your emotions rule and you can be passionate, extreme, and intense. This makes it difficult to act upon reasonable, logical thought. When you are in monkey-brain self, it is as if the threat of the moment (conflict) is as real to you as being face to face with a boa constrictor or some other threat to your life and limb. Your monkey-brain self has taken over your functioning and can flood your system with angry or fearful energy. It can also drain your energy, leading to a feeling of depression. You are most vulnerable to your monkey-brain self taking over when you are sleep deprived, overly stressed, or feeling unhealthy.

When you impulsively act the way you feel while in monkey-brain self, your behavior can become out of control and can negatively impact your relationships. You may have chaotic interactions with others, which can result in hurt feelings that may linger for a long time. Acting in the heat of the moment in monkey-brain self can cause behavior that is irresponsible, careless, mindless, impulsive, and impatient. When emotions are strong, you can distort the facts, magnify excuses, and alter your perception of consequences. High-conflict parenting relationships are particularly vulnerable to moments of acting in monkey-brain self.

In some situations, though, acting from your monkey-brain self can be beneficial, as seen when strong passion intensifies intimate relationships. Serious devotion or desire helps you to persevere with difficult tasks and also to put the needs and safety of others ahead of your own. Mothers who run into the street in traffic to save a child are in monkey-brain self. However, when you can use your reasoning and rationality (fact-and-logic self) together with your intuition and emotion (monkey-brain self), you are harnessing the power and getting the benefit of both states of mind.

Remember what we discussed in chapter 2 about your brain in conflict? As a reminder, when you are in monkey-brain self, you are operating out of the primitive part of the brain that responds to danger with a fight, flight, or freeze reaction. The amygdala is activated. This internal fire alarm has gone off and your brain springs into action, manufacturing chemicals designed to send messages speeding through your nervous system. Like adrenaline, neurotransmitters such as epinephrine and norepinephrine create physiological readiness to deal with an attack, and you are in high alert. In fact, in these moments, the higher, more thoughtful brain functions are not operating. You are in amygdala hijack. Your more primitive brain has hijacked, or taken control over, your ability to reason, think, strategize, and plan.

Facts-and-logic self. Facts-and-logic self is built of facts and common sense. When you are thinking logically and rationally, you are defining reality in terms of facts, numbers, equations, or cause and effect, as described in detail in chapter 2. When you are doing a task such as balancing your checkbook, working on a crossword puzzle, or following your favorite bananabread recipe, you need to be in your facts-and-logic self, paying attention to a sequence of steps and details. The facts-and-logic self is important to learning skills. It's a storehouse of information, almost like your computer's hard drive, which can be called upon to help define a problem objectively, assess options, and determine a solution. Accessing facts-and-logic self is enhanced when you practice self-care by staying healthy, avoiding alcohol and drugs, getting adequate rest, and making healthy nutrition a priority.

Remember back in chapter 2 when we discussed the brain as having three layers? The innermost area, or monkey brain, contains the brainstem and amygdala. The brainstem is considered to be the most primitive part of the brain, and it controls our survival and other instincts. The middle layer, known as the limbic system, controls our emotions, while the outermost layer, the cortex, controls our speech and higher-level thinking skills, such as logic and reasoning. This outer layer, or "bark," of the brain evolved last and expanded a great deal as human beings evolved (Siegel 2009). The facts-and-logic self is associated with the cortex, specifically with brain activity in the left prefrontal cortex. This part of the brain requires a great deal of energy in order to function and needs to have everything just so or it doesn't know what to do. In this part of the brain, goal setting, planning, impulse control, problem solving, visualization, and creative thinking take place. It is deliberate, rational, and "top down."

Centered self. By practicing mindfulness, or observing, you become more capable of accessing the centered self—the balance of your ability to reason with input from your intuition and your emotions. This is critical when dealing with your co-parent. When you can accurately discriminate between states of mind, you can then choose to interact with your co-parenting partner only when you are in your centered self, where you have the greatest chance of "knowing the right thing to do." In this state, your responses are not colored by overwhelming emotions or harsh, critical, or judgmental thoughts as in your monkey-brain self. The centered self is able to respond intuitively and apply common sense that you have come to understand through your life experiences. When you understand what hurts and what helps, you are able to use that understanding to let go of what hurts and strengthen what helps. Accessing our centered self allows us to respond to a situation from a place of wisdom and clarity and draw upon our past experience. Centered self goes beyond knowing your problems and relating your skills to what is hurting you; it transcends all of this by accessing intuition, which grasps the meaning, significance, or truth of an event without tediously having to analyze it. When you are in your centered self, you are able to experience the challenge or problem without adding to it or catastrophizing about it. You do not see it as defining or undermining you or violating your dignity. You are separate from it and can address it as a problem that needs to be solved, looking at the multiple options for a solution without judgment and with a clear head. This can also help you more accurately and compassionately speak to yourself so you are reacting from a better place.

Self-Affirmations for Calmer Co-parenting

Self-affirmations are carefully constructed positive and supportive self-statements that you should write down, put in a conspicuous place where you will see them often, and repeat frequently to yourself. Affirmations are most effective when they are stated in the present tense and are specific, positive, and personal. They can also be linked to your values. When affirmations are stated in the negative, they can drain your power. For example, compare these two affirmations: *I am not so dumb* versus *I'm as smart as I need to be.*

As part of a mindfulness practice to support you in creating a healthy and psychologically safe environment for your children, incorporating value-based affirmations into your daily life can create a constant reminder of your vision and goals. Some examples of value-based affirmations include *I am loving and lovable* and *I am trustworthy.*

The theory behind the power of value-based attributions centers around your basic need to maintain your integrity and sense of adequacy, even if challenged by divorce and conflict. A very common negative attribution about divorce is *I am a failure; I could not make my marriage work.* By focusing on your personal values, you can reconnect with a more expansive view of your "self" and your strengths and capabilities, thus weakening the threat to your personal integrity. One positive affirmation you can give yourself might be *I can teach my children resilience in the face of change.*

Research has found that affirmations improve education, health, and relationship outcomes, with benefits that sometimes persist for months and years (Cohen and Sherman 2014). When you use affirmations, you can experience lasting benefits.

The following statements represent examples of self-affirmations that can support mindfulness in co-parenting and counteract high conflict.

- I want peace for my children as my highest priority.

- I am a loving parent who supports my children in loving both of their parents.

- I love my children more than I hate their other parent.

- I can give my children a parent who teaches them resilience.

- My children deserve peace.

- I can give my children the peace they deserve.

- My children deserve to love and be loved by both of their parents.

- Even though I am divorced, I can give my children the gift of two loving parents.

We hope you have seen how these affirmations differ from the self-blaming and self-critical ways you can speak to yourself. We'd like to help you create and practice your own loving self-statements, which will support you in parenting your children.

Exercise 3.13: Affirmations for Supporting My Children

In this exercise, use the previous examples to create your own affirmations that will remind you of your self-worth and your pledge to protect your children. Try to create a list of at least five affirmations that reflect your own personal values, and remember to state them in positive terms, as if you are already living them.

Once you have written these affirmations in your journal, you can write them again on a separate sheet of paper and put them someplace where you can see them frequently, so you will be easily reminded of your pledges to yourself and your children. How do you feel when you say these affirmations to yourself?

Setting Peaceful Intentions

Setting peaceful and at times loving intentions can also help quiet your emotional response to conflict. Rather than thinking about the stress and the pain, notice what happens if you think about loving and peaceful actions you can take toward yourself and your loved ones. Remember a loving moment with your children, a dear friend, a sibling, or a parent in as much detail as you can. You can use this memory to conjure up that support you felt and calm yourself.

Exercise 3.14: Peaceful and Loving Actions to Quiet My Mind

Think about peaceful and loving actions you can take to help people who are important to you. Jot down the feelings you have as you think about the look on their faces, what they would say, how you would feel. Imagine if you actually followed through and took these actions. You can. How can you bring peace into someone else's life? What can you do to make a difference? Imagine thinking of love and peace as things you do (actions) more than as things you feel (feelings).

Quieting the mind is about *gently* moving away from the thoughts that make you tense. It is not *forcing* yourself not to have the thoughts. Rather, it is about shining the spotlight of your mind onto what is helpful, instead of what is not helpful. This takes practice, as most of us have a mind that is not disciplined and in a sense does what it has been trained to do by others who have been significant to us; often we have believed this was our only way to think since childhood.

But this is not your only choice. You have the ability and options to be harsh and critical, *or* quiet and loving. Which might work better? Indeed, a part of you knows.

A powerful way of addressing chronic conflict with your children's other parent is to cultivate mindfulness and stay attuned to the needs of your children for psychological safety and freedom to love and be loved by both of their parents. Again, you need to pay attention to what is helpful, instead of what is not helpful. This takes practice, as most of us have a mind that is not disciplined. Even if your co-parent will not work together with you, using these tools and skills can help you resist the impulse to be drawn into cycles of conflict that will hurt your children.

Wrapping It Up

In this chapter we have covered a lot of territory, including looking at the mind and how it is differentiated from the brain, and understanding the role of shame and dignity in interactions with your co-parent. We have also looked at the value of having compassion for yourself and your co-parent (and of course your children), and what it means to be a compassionate witness of your own thoughts. You can begin to practice the different methods we've covered for regulating your emotions, including quieting the mind, reciting positive self-affirmations, and consciously setting peaceful intentions, as ways of quieting the conflict with your co-parent. In our next chapter, we will begin to explore the opportunities that are presented in the course of a transition, such as a high-conflict divorce, and what unexpected outcomes may be found.

Taking It Home and Making It Yours

* All people bring their own interpretation to interactions and events as a result of their own set of experiences and personal history. Always assume that your co-parent is responding to any situation based on her own needs and experiences. Although it can be helpful to understand how things appear through your co-parent's eyes, don't get caught up in "watching her movie."

* Be mindful of your own dignity and that of your co-parent. Attempt to resist the temptation to fight one dignity violation with another.

* Incorporate the powerful tool of mindfulness into your life to help you stop your engagement in the cycle of conflict with your co-parent.

* Practice mindfulness in everyday activities as routine as driving, cooking, walking your dog, or washing the dishes.

* Learn to recognize your mind states so that you only engage with your co-parent when you are operating as your centered self. This can significantly reduce your reactivity to the conflict.

* Create your own positive self-affirmations and place them where you can see them frequently to help you remember your goals and values in parenting your children.

* Visualize peaceful moments with loved ones to calm your mind. Create these visualizations by remembering special moments with people you love and painting a vivid picture in your mind. Practice returning to this scene frequently, until you can easily recall it when you need it.

CHAPTER 4

Transforming Yourself from Victim to Survivor to Hero

In this chapter, we will look at the hidden gifts that transitions, such as divorce, can offer, especially the opportunity for profound emotional growth and change. In talking about these growth opportunities, we will discuss the difference between *breaking down* and *breaking open* in the face of life changes (Lesser 2008) and the importance of resilience and rediscovering your true, or authentic, self. We will explore the trap of defining yourself as a victim of divorce, and the impact of that definition on your emerging authentic self. We will also introduce the idea of defining your own core values, reclaiming your authentic self, and learning how to make independent self-appraisals. In doing so, you will explore what it means to take action that is aligned with your core values, regardless of what your co-parent says and does. This process will allow you to increase your self-awareness and experience stability and alignment with your authentic self. The exercises in this chapter are meant to help you develop a healthier way of viewing yourself and to find emotional separation from your ex-spouse, while staying fully engaged as a co-parent for the sake of your children.

The Gifts of Transition

Change and transition are inevitable in our lives. Building resilience in the face of change is a skill that serves us well at any age and throughout our life cycle. Resilience gives you the feeling that you are always wearing your "life vest" and always prepared to swim and not sink. An added benefit of building your own resilience is the ability to model and teach this skill to your children. Learning to be resilient at a young age can endow your children with a life-long skill that buffers and protects them from falling apart in the face of inevitable losses and transitions over the course of their lifetime.

When you have exercised and built the "muscles" that enable you to ride the waves of change with a feeling of safety and resilience, you are more prepared for whatever transitions are ahead. Some transitions are expected, like the ending of a school year and going from one grade to the next or one school to the next. You anticipate and plan and prepare for these transitions. These transitions are supported and celebrated by your families and your institutions and are sometimes even marked with rituals and ceremonies, like graduations.

Then there are other transitions that are sudden, unexpected, and unwelcome, like the news that you or a dear friend or relative has been diagnosed with a terminal illness, or your spouse telling you that he or she no longer wants to be married to you, or your boss terminating your employment unexpectedly, or the sudden death of someone important in your life. Transitions like these often dislodge your life in a profound way and leave you in a place of uncertainty and disruption, overwhelmed with feelings of anxiety, sadness, anger, fear, and perhaps grief and despair.

When you are deeply entrenched in the routines of your life, you often do not have the impetus or motivation to think about whether you are fully yourself or just going through the motions in your life. You may be holding on to deep pain and grief from emotional wounds or bruises in your childhood, which are hidden from you as you go about your day-to-day life. You may have even chosen your partner with the unconscious wish that he would heal those hurts, and over the years found that his own wounds and bruises make it impossible for him to heal yours, and for you to heal his.

The transition of a divorce can offer the opportunity to stop living on autopilot and attend to wounds and bruises you have long ignored, opening up the possibility of deep healing, personal growth, and profound, meaningful change. In the pursuit of such growth, you can find strength and resilience and learn to cope with adversity in ways you never knew existed. Building this resiliency and connecting to your authentic self and your strength can be a powerful model of coping and recovery for your children. It can leave you as a stronger individual and parent than you were before.

With transitions comes choice: you may approach them by either breaking down or by breaking open (Lesser 2008).

Breaking Down

Breaking down occurs when you are overwhelmed with emotional pain and do everything you can to avoid those feelings. This can lead you to cease functioning, perhaps spending days in bed and withdrawing from your activities, friends, and community, or perhaps becoming endlessly busy, allowing you to avoid the changes and challenges you are facing. Sometimes breaking down leads to self-medicating with drugs or alcohol, gambling, excessive shopping, and other excesses as you try to cope. Despair can set in and the fallout from your isolation or self-medication can intensify, sending you into darkness, a tailspin, or a free-fall. It can be difficult to climb back out of this dark hole. It is particularly important to note that your children are witness to your emotional state. For children, living with a parent who is breaking down can be scary and feel very unsafe.

When you are in this state, you and your children need physical and emotional safety. It may be necessary for another adult, such as a family member, friend, or childcare helper, to step in and stabilize routines for your children, especially if they are young. If you are in a state of breaking down, you will need as much support as possible from your community, employer, family, and friends. Medical or mental health intervention may be necessary to help restore you to more stable functioning.

Breaking Open

While breaking down and breaking open might look similar on the surface, those who *break open* are not walling themselves off from the pain, but rather embracing it and allowing themselves to feel it and sit with it without fear. When you break open in the face of transition, you allow yourself to feel all of the myriad feelings you have, without avoiding or denying their existence. You are open to all the turmoil and disruption, and not afraid to let it wash over you. You may need to wail; talk it out with your family, friends, and medical or mental health professionals for guidance; or rely on your religious beliefs to help you through the difficult moments, but you do not push them away, deny them, self-medicate, or create so much busyness to avoid acknowledging them. Breaking open creates significant opportunity to bring wounds from the past to the surface and allow them to heal. The experience of dislocation and disruption from your routines can be used to help you recognize buried wounds and bruises and attend to them in a conscious way.

Exercise 4.1: Did I Break Down or Did I Break Open?

Think about your own response to the life transition of your divorce. How did you approach it? Did you break down, or break open? What did that look like? How did you feel at the time? If you are now looking in the rearview mirror, what does it look like from this perspective? Have you found that you were able to grow in the process? Write down what helped you grow. What helped you adjust? What helped you be resilient and recover? Was it just time, or was it something else? Do you see ways that you can harvest more growth from this experience?

Developing Safety Zones

Whether you have broken down or broken open, it is likely that there has been disruption in your familiar routines. In order to ensure safety, in other words to make your world calmer and more secure, it is critical to reestablish familiar routines or create new ones. Routines can be established in these different aspects of your daily life.

Spiritual: To help ground you in your connection to the bigger universe, you can reconnect with your own preferred expression of spirituality through any number of channels, be it a spiritual leader, a special friend, a meaningful book or passage, a familiar ritual, a place of worship, or a favorite setting in nature.

Mental: By doing things that reaffirm your self-esteem and self-worth, you can remind yourself of your value. You might find this by connecting with a special person, group, or team or by participating in an activity that makes you feel good about yourself. You might also experience this by doing something that helps others, like volunteering in a soup kitchen or hospital.

Vocational: Become mindful of the value of your work, and maintain your schedule and activities to the extent possible. If you need to make changes in your work (for instance, if your primary work has been in your home and you will need to seek employment elsewhere), begin to envision the steps to prepare yourself for work that will be meaningful and satisfying. Don't hesitate to seek help and guidance if you need to restart or change vocations.

Financial: To develop financial stability, it is critical to fully understand your finances and get control of them. Becoming mindful of your sources of income, assets, debt, and spending is the first step to creating realistic plans for your current and future economic life.

Social: To be in touch with a feeling of belonging, it is important to maintain connections to friends and community. If you have withdrawn from or neglected those ties, it is helpful to reconnect.

Apologize freely if you have been in "hiding," and seek relationships that are supportive and healthy (not full of intrigue or drama).

Familial: To access the support of your family, it is helpful to maintain consistent contact and relationships with significant family members. Be sure to have conversations that are about them and not just about your situation. In fact, it can be helpful to tell family (and friends) that you do not want to talk about your co-parent, as those discussions can easily revert back to the "war" and what you should or shouldn't do.

Physical: To have the strength and energy to deal with your current situation and your future, it is critical to maintain or develop healthy patterns of sleep, exercise, and nutrition and be consistent in following them. You don't have to measure success or set rigid goals. Just allow yourself the opportunity to take good care of your body. Be conscious and mindful of how you eat, exercise, and move.

Exercise 4.2: My Safety Zones

Go through each of your safety zones and evaluate where you are in each sphere of your life.

Spiritual

Mental

Vocational

Financial

Social

Familial

Physical

Look at each one separately. Where do you need to improve to create more safety? For each sphere of safety, write down what aspects are going well and what needs improvement. Rate yourself in each sphere as Deeply Satisfied, Satisfied, Needs Improvement, or Isn't Working. This can help you pinpoint areas in which to focus or concentrate to build greater balance.

Now, make a plan for how you will create more safety in any of these areas where you did not feel you had adequate safety in place. Think of what resources you have in each area to help you make your plan if you feel stuck. Who can be your partner in this planning? Who can help you in an overall safety plan, or in each of the specific areas? You can make another list of the safety zones and next to each one write a plan to create more safety for yourself.

Some areas you may choose to work on by yourself. The point is creating zones of safety and comfort that you can use routinely or just when needed to make your world calmer and more secure.

You Are Not a Victim of Your Divorce

How you define yourself affects how you deal with difficult and challenging circumstances and situations. When you see yourself as a helpless victim of a situation, you can become passive and powerless. The more you become paralyzed in the face of a danger or challenge, or continue to protest how unreasonable, unfair, and threatening the situation is without taking appropriate action to change it, the more you are putting yourself in a passive, childlike role, compounding the damage and stifling your opportunity to adapt and grow. Similarly, when you are preoccupied with what is "fair" or "right," or the way things "should" be, you can find yourself in a position of holding on to anger, being righteously indignant, boiling inside, and feeling vengeful and justified but stuck in your bitterness. The victim role is maladaptive, even when the things that have happened to you have been horrid and hurtful, beyond your control and difficult to understand. When you see yourself as a victim, you rob yourself of your power to move forward—and ultimately to heal.

If you have been hurt or betrayed by your partner, you may be holding on to the victim role. What you may not see is that staying in this role is hurtful to your self and your soul, not to mention your children and their safe passage through this transition. Staying stuck in the role of victim does not allow you to access the gifts of transition and the opportunities for healing and recovery along with growth and development of your authentic self. Sometimes, it is even hard to see if you are in the role of the victim.

Exercise 4.3: Am I Seeing Myself as a Victim?

Many of us emerge from childhood having experienced a parent who was in some way in the role of a victim. Without even knowing it, we may be as well. To assess whether you are casting yourself into the role of victim of your divorce, ask yourself whether the following statements are true for you.

Do you believe your aggression against your ex-spouse is justified because of the ways he has treated you?

Do you find it difficult to take responsibility for your own happiness or misery?

Does it seem like your ex-spouse is responsible for all of your suffering and pain?

Do you nag, complain, and harass your ex-spouse until she gives in to your demands?

Do you provoke aggressive behavior from your ex-spouse, and then downplay or ignore your role in it?

If you have answered yes to any of these questions, you may be hampering your own growth by casting yourself in the role of victim and limiting your power to take charge of your healing and recovery. If you recognize that you have cast yourself as a victim of your divorce, you can use this knowledge to become more mindful about how you are interpreting situations with your ex-spouse and how you are reacting to these situations based upon your interpretation.

Set an intention to consciously examine each situation from the vantage point of understanding your own role and looking for what you can change and control in your own actions and reactions. This will help you take the first step toward moving away from a victim mentality. Pay mindful attention to whether you are operating from your centered self in interactions with your co-parent, and create strategies and opportunities that allow you to stop and think before you react (to the email, text, or phone call).

Tune in to the emotions (anger, fear, sadness) that accompany your feelings of victimization and develop an awareness of the feelings that signal that you're getting caught up in feeling victimized. These emotions can be a cue for you to challenge your view when you find yourself operating from a victim mentality. If you find that the victim stance is no longer serving you well, you may wish to get help to change this way of looking at the world, perhaps through individual or group therapy, a support group, or individual coaching. As you seek to transition out of a victim role, it is helpful to uncover your authentic self. The first step toward finding or creating your authentic self is an exploration of your core values.

Core Values

Your *core values* are the fundamental personal beliefs that you hold true. These are the beliefs that define who you are as a person and how you respond to challenges and life when you are listening to your authentic self. Redefining or rediscovering your core values is essential to being more aware of your authentic self. Being mindful of your core values allows you to operate in tune with your centered self. In this section, we will be examining a representative set of core values. You can choose which ones mean the most to you so that you can solidify your own individual set of core values that speak most loudly to you. It is critical to hold on to your self during and after a divorce process, or to reclaim a self that you have lost. As you transition from your status as part of a married couple to that of a separate person and single parent, having a clear knowledge of your core values as an individual and a parent will help center you. You can bring your authentic self out into the sunshine, away from the darkness of a difficult marriage.

Defining Your Core Values as an Individual

In thinking of yourself as an independent entity, separate and apart from your parents, siblings, children, ex-spouse, friends, coworkers, neighbors, and others, it is helpful to define your core values—those that truly represent who you are and motivate you. This next exercise will help you define those values.

Exercise 4.4: Defining My Core Values as an Individual

Below is a representative list of core values to choose from. The list is from the Values Clarification Worksheet in *Emotion Efficacy Therapy* (McKay and West 2016). This is not an exhaustive list, but likely encompasses many if not all of the critical categories. Choose up to five values that are your defining values as an individual. Feel free to add values that are important to you if you do not see them on this list.

Accountability	Contribution	Excellence
Accuracy	Control	Excitement
Achievement	Cooperation	Expertise
Adventure	Correctness	Exploration
Altruism	Courtesy	Expressiveness
Ambition	Creativity	Fairness
Assertiveness	Curiosity	Faith
Authenticity	Decisiveness	Family
Balance	Dependability	Fitness
Belonging	Determination	Fluency
Boldness	Devoutness	Focus
Calmness	Diligence	Freedom
Carefulness	Discipline	Friends
Challenge	Discretion	Fun
Cheerfulness	Diversity	Generosity
Clear-mindedness	Dynamism	Grace
Commitment	Economy	Growth
Community	Effectiveness	Happiness
Compassion	Efficiency	Hard work
Competitiveness	Elegance	Health
Consistency	Empathy	Helping
Contentment	Enjoyment	Holiness
Continuous improvement	Enthusiasm	Honesty
	Equality	Honor

Humility

Independence

Ingenuity

Inner harmony

Inquisitiveness

Insightfulness

Intellectual status

Intelligence

Intuition

Joy

Justice

Leadership

Legacy

Love

Loyalty

Making a
difference

Mastery

Merit

Obedience

Openness

Order

Originality

Patriotism

Piety

Positivity

Practicality

Preparedness

Professionalism

Prudence

Quality

Reliability

Resourcefulness

Restraint

Results-oriented

Rigor

Security

Self-actualization

Self-control

Self-reliance

Selflessness

Sensitivity

Serenity

Service

Shrewdness

Simplicity

Soundness

Speed

Spontaneity

Stability

Strength

Structure

Success

Support

Teamwork

Temperance

Thankfulness

Thoroughness

Thoughtfulness

Timeliness

Tolerance

Tradition

Trustworthiness

Truth-seeking

Understanding

Uniqueness

Unity

Usefulness

Vision

Vitality

Here is an example:

My core values are:

1. Responsibility

2. Self-sufficiency

3. Self-worth

4. Authenticity

5. Compassion

Now choose *your* core values and list them in your journal.

What do you notice about your choices? What do they say about you as a person? How are they similar to or different from what you imagine your parents would say about their own core values? During your marriage, were you living in a way that was consistent with these values? What changes do you need to make to live in a way that is consistent with your core values as you move into your future?

Defining Your Core Values as a Parent

Once you have looked at your core values as an individual, it is valuable to look at how you define yourself as a parent, and if at all possible, to look at the values of your co-parent, to determine what the central forces behind each member of the team supporting and raising your children are. Ideally, these are the values you wish to nurture and develop in your children.

Exercise 4.5: Defining My Core Values as a Parent

In your journal, list your core values as a parent, using the representative list from exercise 4.4 as a guide.

Next, list the values you imagine your co-parent would list as his or her core values as a parent.

Clearly defining your core values can lead you to more of an understanding of your authentic self. And keeping in mind your co-parent's view of his core values can help you respond with more understanding, even when he has flipped his lid.

Now let's look at the difference between a false self and an authentic self.

Discovery of the Authentic Self

D. W. Winnicott (1960), a well-known pediatrician and psychoanalyst, wrote about the concepts of the "true self" and "the false self." Essentially, your false self is a way of being that is based upon meeting other people's needs and expectations. It is developed very early in life when your parents are not attuned or able to respond to your needs as an infant, and you instead have to be attuned to the needs of your parent. As a result, you develop a "self" that makes other people's expectations and needs more important than your own and relies on others to define yourself. This may have been reinforced when you were a young child and got smiles and praise for doing what pleased your parents. Many of us spend too much time living as false selves, to get praise from those we value, without awareness that this false self is hiding our true or authentic self. This can cause our day-to-day experience to feel empty and not real. Conversely, when you are operating from your authentic self, you are experiencing what it feels like to be alive, to simply be, accepting of your limitations and vulnerabilities, and acting spontaneously from your center. When you are your authentic self, your self-image is aligned with your goals, beliefs, values, words, and behavior.

When you are embroiled in high conflict with your co-parent, it is likely that you are not in tune with your authentic self. If you were primed in childhood to operate from a false self, it is likely that you entered your marriage in this way, perhaps more focused on your spouse's responses than your own feelings, needs, and views. Our goal here is to help you shed the false self that you likely lived in during your marriage, which has followed you into your postdivorce life, and connect with your authentic self. When you do this, you are more able to access your centered self and interact from that place when dealing with your co-parent. You are then less likely to experience an amygdala hijack and react with fight, flight, or freeze. Instead, you can maintain your dignity and respond from your centered self with access to all of your reason and emotions.

Exercise 4.6: Using My Core Values to Deal with Conflict

Think about a recent conflict with your co-parent. In your journal, describe the situation and how you responded. Next, rewrite a response that is "centered" and operating from your authentic self. Speak from your core values as an individual *and* as a parent. What differences do you notice? Do you feel differently when responding this way? When you find yourself in a conflict with your co-parent, ask yourself whether you are operating from your authentic self. Reacting in a centered way can help you avoid having an emotional reaction. It can instead help you maintain your dignity and protect your children from another emotional storm.

Transforming from Victim to Hero Through Narrative Work

You are the creator of your own narrative about the events in your life. You are the author of these stories and can tell them from different perspectives and angles, emphasizing different aspects of them. You can tell your stories with yourself as the victim of your experiences. Yet, at the same time, you have the power to recast your own stories in ways that are growth producing and empowering. Consider our colleague's story:

Amy's Story

Amy's second husband stole her life savings. She now says she will have to work until she's 95. As a mental health professional, she was mortified and said that she was so stupid to have married a sociopath. She repeatedly asked, "How could I not have seen this coming? How could I have let myself be duped? How could I not have awoken sooner? How could someone I loved so much betray the trust I placed in him?" She felt miserable and depressed. The "story" she told herself was basically *I'm a stupid loser.*

One day Amy met another man whom she unquestionably calls "the love of my life." Then, after a time, it dawned on her: Perhaps the marriage to the sociopath had to be so bad that she was left with no choice but to end it in order to find the right partner. She was no longer "the loser" but someone who had to go through a very difficult and trying journey in order to get to the other side. She changed her story, or narrative, and that changed her emotional experience. Her former spouse did not change, and she did not get her life savings back. But the new way in which she told her story was self-affirming, allowed her dignity, and made sense of the value of her experience.

The difference was that the new story that Amy crafted in her mind led to better emotional, and in all likelihood physical, feelings. Joan Borysenko (personal communication, October 4, 2014) speaks to this, saying that we write the stories of our life. She explains that we always have the option to rewrite the story, since we are the author of the story in the first place.

In chapter 3, we asked you to look at what you blame your ex-spouse for, what your ex-spouse blames you for, and your emotional responses to those narratives. We asked you to separate yourself from the views of your ex-spouse and recognize that they are not you, but only the views of someone else who you were perhaps allowing to define you and therefore allowing to cause you emotional distress. Earlier in this chapter, you had a chance to look at whether you define yourself as a victim. Choosing to resist defining yourself as a victim, and committing to redefine yourself from a position of strength, will open you to new ways of approaching potentially conflictual situations with your co-parent. Defining your core values and finding your authentic self gives you opportunities to see yourself more clearly through your own lens (rather than that of your co-parent), hold on to your dignity, and protect yourself from being provoked into reactions that are not productive and cause you to feel shame. In the next section, we are going to provide an opportunity to change your story so you can shift your experience from one of a victim to that of a survivor, and even a hero.

A Hero's Journey

As we fumble through our lives, we are all in the midst of a journey, not knowing ultimately where it will take us. In rewriting the story of your divorce, you have the opportunity to reframe your story to one that empowers you. In retelling your story, you can focus on resilience and transforming yourself from victim to hero. By doing so, you can move from being in "pieces" to being in "peace" (Joan Borysenko, October 5, 2014).

Joseph Campbell (2008), a scholar of mythology, speaks about "the hero's journey," which comprises three stages. These stages can be applied to the task of rewriting your divorce story and changing the story of your postdivorce life.

Stage one involves "separation from the known." In this stage of the story, there is some kind of crisis. Something difficult has happened in your life. In telling the story of your divorce, this stage would involve the events leading up to the moment you realize that your marriage is unraveling and that your separation and divorce was inevitable.

In the second stage of the journey, you are in the "moment of uncertainty"—the time between "no longer" and "not yet." This is often a stage in which you feel dislodged and adrift. Your familiar roles have been challenged and have fallen away. You may feel as if you have lost your bearings and the bottom has fallen out of your life. In this stage, the predominant emotion is one of shock and grief. In looking for support through this stage, you may draw upon the strength of other people who become allies and mentors. You may also find that there are people in your life who are not supporting your growth. These "friends" often drop out of the picture. At some level, these people are opponents of our growth. This stage in your divorce story occurs in the days and months (perhaps years) following the decision to divorce, and lasts through, and perhaps beyond, the process that legally unties your marriage.

The third stage takes place when you have "gone through the fire" and you return to your life as the authentic or true version of yourself. If you have been transformed by your experience and can turn your "wounds into wisdom" and turn your "garbage into compost," you are in a position to live authentically and inspire others as well (Joan Borysenko, personal communication, October 5, 2014).

In this next exercise, we are going to give you an opportunity to rewrite your own divorce story, paying attention to the three stages in the hero's journey. We would like you to think about what you experienced in each of the stages, and write with as much detail as you can.

Exercise 4.7: Retelling My
Divorce Story as a Hero's Journey

Write the story of your divorce in the present tense, with vivid detail and as much feeling as you can. Write about it in three stages as described above: "separation from the known," "moment of uncertainty," and having "gone through the fire" (Campbell 2008). Retell your story, consciously focusing on aspects of resilience and growth that emerged from your experience. Be sure to spend time on the third stage. What did you feel as you went through the third stage? What did you learn?

Retelling your story as a hero's journey can help you focus on the elements of growth and on your future. What does it feel like for you to tell your story from this perspective? Does it feel different, more empowering? Can you see opportunities for healing and growth? Can you use this story in your daily life to motivate you to face your fears, try new things, and use your voice? Do you see resilience in yourself that you can harness to deal with other difficult and challenging situations and transitions? When you see yourself as a hero, does it give you more hope and optimism going forward? Can you start to let go of reactivity to your co-parent's criticism or blame? Can you see that her comments are *hers* and don't define you? Can you hear the criticism as just your co-parent's opinion, not a statement of fact? You are who you are, regardless of someone else's thoughts, disappointment, and disapproval.

Wrapping It Up

In this chapter, we explored some very powerful concepts, beginning with the unexpected gifts of transition. Developing the resilience to approach expected and unexpected transitions with openness and curiosity will allow you to take full advantage of the opportunities and hidden possibilities for growth and change. The series of questions we posed in exercise 4.3 helped you assess whether you are operating from the perspective of a victim. If you are, you can use the approaches discussed in this chapter to change this perspective, which include defining or redefining your core values as you seek to recover your authentic self. Creating this list of core values can bring you more in touch with your authentic self, which will then allow you to approach your co-parent from the more centered position we discussed in chapter 3. Finally, rewriting your divorce story as a hero's journey is another, deeper way of transforming the way you see yourself—from victim to survivor to hero.

Taking It Home and Making It Yours

* Understand the gifts of transition and open yourself to the growth opportunities that transition can offer.

* Create awareness of whether you have become stuck in a victim mentality. If you find that you have, challenge this way of looking at your situation with the help of friends, family, or professionals.

* Look to become your authentic self as an individual and as a parent by defining and focusing on your core values.

* Rewrite your divorce story as a hero's journey, focusing on your growth, strength, and resilience, and what you've learned through this transition.

PART 2

Your Journey as a Co-Parent

CHAPTER 5

Parental Conflict

As we have discussed, chronic parental conflict is one of the most difficult aspects of divorce for children and for parents. Where does it come from? One thought is that conflict is a response to a perceived attack on your ego. In this chapter we will first discuss the ego. Then we will look at patterns of conflict, how emotions impact conflict, and ideas for reducing conflict. We will also discuss how to prepare for and react effectively to conflict and how to recover from conflict with your co-parent.

The Ego

The term *ego* describes your sense of self—your attitudes, values, and concerns. It is that sense of who you are as a person, or what some refer to as self-worth. That is not your actual worth, but your own view of your worth.

When you were a young child, much of your sense of self came from your experiences with your parents. How did they treat you? Were they loving and considerate? Were you often disregarded or ignored? Did they praise and compliment you? Were you often blamed or criticized? Did they show that they believed in you? As a child, you likely internalized these experiences and defined your value by the reactions of those around you (most likely your parents) who explained the rest of your world to you. As you grew, this tendency to look to others to define yourself probably broadened to friends and then to romantic partners.

During courtship, you may have experienced the intoxicating effect of romance and said to yourself, *I'm in love. My partner adores me. I'm worth a million bucks.* Contrast this with a breakup: *My partner dumped me. I'm no good. No one will ever love me. I'm garbage.*

As your marriage failed, your ego may have been greatly impacted. It is so easy to interpret the failing of the marriage as related to self-worth. You might have ask yourself questions such as:

Why wasn't I lovable enough for my partner?

How could I have picked someone who was so wrong for me?

How could I have been so stupid to not see this coming?

How can I possibly stay in this marriage without dying inside?

If this could happen to me, who will ever love me?

How can I do this to my children?

What kind of person am I?

Why couldn't I just make this work?

How could I have messed up my marriage?

These kinds of questions expose your ego and your self-evaluation to being determined by the situation and relationship experiences of both your marriage and your divorce. The pain from this view of yourself can be intense and can be triggered and then repeatedly retriggered by even the simplest of events.

For example, your co-parent's being ten minutes late to pick up or drop off the children can be incredibly emotionally provocative. It might symbolize another disregard for "me" (and the children) if you interpret it as *Again, he is keeping me waiting? How can he treat me like this? It is no different now from when we were married.* Look at how you interpret your co-parent's behavior in a way that connects directly with your self-worth. It is as if the person who is late is in some way defining the value or worth of the person who is waiting by virtue of being late. The person who is waiting has given away her own sense of self to the actions of her co-parent. And, notice how she has given away her sense of self to someone she probably does not particularly like or trust.

Switch the scenario. If the plumber you called to fix the leaky faucet is ten minutes late, you may get mildly miffed, but you probably wouldn't relate this to your self-worth. The worker is just late. You may even be glad that the plumber simply showed up—late or not. Or, you might be glad he was late if you were rushing to be ready for him to arrive.

You can take your ego out of the equation in the first example by shifting your interpretation of your co-parent's behavior, for example by saying something such as *He is late again. This is nothing new. It was the same when we were married. It is just the way he is.* Notice how the comments are not about you; they don't include the word *me*. They are just comments that recognize the behavior, without explaining or personalizing it. Let's now apply this to your specific interactions with your co-parent.

Exercise 5.1: Getting the Ego Out of It

(One last reminder: you can download this and all the exercises in this book at http://www.newharbinger.com/39041.)

In your journal, make a list of three behaviors of your former partner that get you emotionally activated or upset. Next, for each behavior, write down what that behavior means to you. What does your co-parent think about you that would lead to that behavior?

Next, change that narrative to one that has nothing to do with you. Just describe your co-parent's behaviors without relating these actions to your worth. Lastly, write how you feel when you do not personalize the actions of your former partner.

As you think about your divorce, you still might say, "I get all that, but this is *my* divorce. How could it not be about me? My life is turned upside down. My dreams shattered. My future is uncertain. My children are falling apart. How could this not be about me?"

Of course, divorce feels like it is *about* you. However, we find it helpful to think of divorce as an experience you are going through, rather than something that *defines* you. This is an important distinction. Divorce is a very stressful life event—but not something that defines your character or inner essence. The comments of your spouse, the events that have happened, and the betrayal of trust are challenges to deal with. They are part of your story or journey (see chapter 4) but are not about your value as a person.

When you internalize a situation and make what someone else does or does not do about you, your ego (or sense of self) gets involved. In fact, there is an old saying, "Conflict is an attack on the self." When you have *internal* conflict, you are often upset with yourself and in a state of dis-equilibrium (or dis-ease). When you have *external* conflict, you are often upset with someone else (and often yourself as well). At these times, the dis-ease can escalate into all-out attack and defensiveness.

This can play out if you reverse the scenario and your co-parent says to you, "I can't believe you were late again. What's wrong with you? Is your precious job more important than the children? You'll never change!" It is pretty hard to fend off the sense that this is a personal attack. The key is what you do with the attack. Do you let it in? Do you give the attacker credibility? Do you allow your sense of self or ego to be hurt by the attack? If so, then you are likely to move into a defensive posture and return fire (or fight) by saying something such as "Oh, you're talking about my being late? What about last week when you were forty-five minutes late, 'because of traffic.' Yeah right. Traffic. Really? Even the kids didn't believe that. And, by the way, in case you forgot, my job brings in a big share of the income for the kids. Are you going to step up to the plate and take over that responsibility? Oh sure. I'll just quit my job."

Or, do you take a different approach and decide to simply end the barrage, hang up, and not return texts and emails? Do you "block" your co-parent and decide to not interact with someone who can be so emotionally harsh and possibly abusive? This avoidance (or flight) response is also very common and easy to fall into when you interpret the actions and comments of the other as an attack on your core sense of self.

Whether you choose fight or flight, this kind of responding continues the conflict by defining the actions of your co-parent as demeaning and threatening to your own sense of self.

Exercise 5.2: Getting Over Fight or Flight

In your journal, list some examples of times in which you engaged in the fight. What was the situation? What was the issue? How did you fight?

Next, list some examples of times when you decided to be in the flight mode. What was the situation? What was the issue? How did you flee?

Now go back over these situations and see if you can, simply from a practical perspective, offer a solution to each situation, as if you were a third party who had no investment in who won or lost, but were simply addressing the issue at hand and trying to find a reasonable solution. By not defining the situation as being related to your self-worth, and instead looking at it as a practical problem to address, you can handle it with less of an emotional (and corresponding physical) reaction.

Cycles of Conflict

Looking at conflict from the outside, you can often see distinct patterns. It can be helpful to step back and recognize the types of conflict that are prevalent in interactions with your co-parent. Being able to label cycles of conflict can help give you some distance, rather than just feeling caught up in them. People who meditate often find this strategy helpful for dealing with the uncomfortable physical and emotional experiences that can happen during prolonged meditation. Saying to yourself, *Why is my nose itching?* or *Why am I sad?* often leads to more discomfort. Instead, simply labeling, *My nose is itching* or *Hmm, sadness* can lead to the experience or the feeling passing. Zen masters might describe this as a leaf floating by on a stream. We don't have to personalize the leaf, or under-stand why or how it got there. We can simply notice it, and as it floats by, also notice the glistening water. We can notice that some of the leaves are similar to one another, while others are uniquely different. Let's look at the types of leaves (or cycles) that have the word *conflict* written on them.

Downward Spiral

One type of conflictual cycle is a *downward spiral*. The conflict sometimes begins in a subtle or nuanced way, and slowly escalates with each step getting a bit more intense and blatant until the two people are at war again. We see this in many types of arguments when parents who were initially interacting normally begin to spiral down. It can begin over rather trivial issues or with an off-handed remark and then escalate into intensely upsetting experiences. This may have happened in the marriage as well, and might have led to what some couples call "great make-ups." In divorce, while the pattern of having intensely negative interactions occurs, there usually is little to no making up. Instead resentment builds as each of you may add yet one more insult to your inventory of grievances about your co-parent. This downward spiral can relate to attachment seeking (chapter 6), as one parent knows that if he wants to get the other parent's attention, the easiest and most efficient way to do so is to be negative and provocative. Who better to push one's buttons than a former partner?

Negative Intimacy

In this cycle of conflict, we see one or both parents engage in very personal and intense communication as you might find in an intimate relationship; however, it is negative and unpleasant and often takes the form of a heated argument. There may not be a downward spiral operat-ing here, but just an ongoing pattern of hostile interactions that occur over and over about a variety of small and large issues (Ricci 1997).

These intensely negative interactions seem to keep a kind of passion in the relationship, even though the arguments are extremely unpleasant. When there is *negative intimacy*, we often see the same amount of energy applied to the argument about where to drop off a child on a given day, for example, as to the argument related to making a difficult and complex medical decision on behalf of your child. Each of these situations and the arguments about them lead to intense negative emotion and conflict.

Linking

A third kind of conflictual cycle is one we call *linking*. Here we see multiple issues or objections that get connected to one another. If one issue surfaces, the conflict erupts as each decision or action hinges on the other. This is evident in scenarios such as the following:

Jack: Will you give me the passports for the children? I want to take them out of the country.

Janice: I will give you the passports when you start to give me the child support payments on time.

Jack: That's ridiculous. I don't give you the payments on time because you never give me your share of unreimbursed medical expenses.

Janice: Why would I do that, when you don't pay your share of the extracurricular expenses?

How can the conflict end when these issues are all linked to one another? Who will budge? Why would they budge? Jack and Janice have built an almost ironclad way of staying in conflict by having every issue connected to another.

The different kinds of cycles of conflict described above can lead parents to engage in bitter conflict for years after the divorce and even for years after the children are grown. As mentioned in chapter 1, this has been called *conflict addiction* (Thayer and Zimmerman 2001). Such parents don't attend life-cycle events such as graduations, weddings, and births of grandchildren together. They say things like "If [that parent] is going to be there, then I am not. You know I can't be in the same room as your [father/mother]." Children and even grandchildren are impacted by the conflict that can easily be twenty to thirty years old.

Exercise 5.3: Assessing My Cycles of Conflict

Think about the three cycles of conflict we have just discussed. In your journal, write down examples of each type as it applies to your relationship with your former partner. Which types of cycles occur repeatedly? What is your role in the cycle of conflict? What might you do differently? How might you react in a way that does not escalate the conflict but rather simply addresses the practical issue that is in dispute? Naming and labeling the types of conflict helps you to do this by allowing you to distance yourself from the conflict.

Emotions and Conflict

The cycles of conflict are directly tied to emotions. These emotional factors prime the pump and make you more susceptible to reacting to the words and actions of the other parent. They, in a sense, keep you tuned in to and on the lookout for the "battle." They can even lead to you seeing a battle when it might not even be the intent of your co-parent to have such a battle. We see this in healthy relationships when two people who care deeply for one another get into an argument and then stop and look at each other. One then says, "I don't know how that happened. I didn't want to fight with you," and the other says, "I didn't want to fight with you either." The couple got caught up in their assumptions and reactions to each other. In conflictual relationships, it is almost impossible for this not to occur.

However, imagine if you did not have a history with the other parent. Imagine if you were (as if in a science-fiction movie) simply assigned to each other to raise the children. Imagine if you did not have any "baggage" or uncomfortable feelings toward your co-parent. Would you be freer? Would a weight be lifted?

Instead, you may hold on to a lot of psychological dynamics and emotions from the relationship (and possibly the litigation). Let's look at some of them in an attempt to first understand them, and then to possibly decide what to let go of, or let float away as a leaf on the stream.

Holding On to Anger

Divorce can lead to exquisite levels of emotional pain. This often gets experienced as anger. However, there is a Buddhist quote about anger that says, "Holding onto anger is like grasping a hot coal with the intent of throwing it at someone else; you are the one who gets burned." Some former spouses transact most interactions through anger. This form of intense, negative passion can dominate your interactions with each other and seriously impact your children as they get caught in the middle of the conflict and hear their parents disparaging each other. We have actually heard parents speak to us in confidence of their continued love for the other parent, while publicly verbally bashing each other. Is expressing the anger truly helpful? Whom does it really help? Who gets burned?

Holding On to the Past

Conflict can often be exacerbated when you revert back to the past. You use the past to predict the future and to justify your positions in the present. You may say, "You never were interested in doing that before; why would I think you'd be interested now?" At other times, you can dispute what your co-parent is saying in the present by a statement such as "During our court battle you said those horrible things about my parenting. Now you're trying to say I'm a good parent. Yeah right." Arguments can then develop about the validity of the interpretation or even the comment about the past when your co-parent says, "It didn't happen that way" or "I never said that." Holding on to the past can also lead to one parent's previous mistakes being used as the precedent for the other's future actions. For example, one parent might say, "Last Thanksgiving you didn't accommodate my request to change the schedule, so why should I accommodate your request now?" Holding on to the past provides plenty of fuel for the fire of conflict and creates a pile of hot rocks that will burn your hand.

Holding On to the Truth

The "truth" is very elusive. In an experiment conducted in an introduction to psychology course, a stranger unexpectedly runs into the lecture hall, grabs the professor's briefcase, and runs out. The 100 students in the room are then asked to describe the person who took the briefcase. Invariably something that happened just moments ago and in plain view of the entire class is described inconsistently by those present. The witnesses have many different descriptions of the "thief."

When it comes to parenting, you will, when alone with your child, confront your child when he is distorting the truth or is outright lying. "You really did all your homework in just ten minutes?" In these instances, you strongly doubt that your child is telling the truth, or you know he is lying.

However, when your child brings your co-parent into a conversation, there is often an instant acceptance of your child's version of the truth. A five-year-old told his father that he did not have dinner on Sunday at his mother's. The father asked the mother, "Is it your habit not to feed our child dinner?" The father believed he knew the truth based on what he heard from his son. The mother thought for a moment and simply said, "Sunday? Oh yes. My folks were over. We had a mid-afternoon large meal. I gave Timmy a snack around 7 p.m. Technically he is right. He did not have 'dinner' at 6 p.m. because he ate at 3:30 and then had a snack at 7 p.m." In this case Timmy was not knowingly distorting the truth. He just had a perception that we can understand, given his age, as he did not sit down in the kitchen and have the usual dinner meal at around 6 p.m. The conflict, though, begins when the parent unconditionally believes that the information reported by the child is the absolute truth, then interprets it in a way that is most damning to the other parent and is convinced that there can be no other explanation.

Holding On to Being Right

There is a saying, "Would you rather be right, or at peace?" Think about how much energy goes into trying to prove to someone who is not open to it that he is wrong and you are right. At the same time, he is likely to be trying to prove just how wrong you are. This does not lead to resolution, as both of you are defending your positions in an adversarial manner and perhaps looking for the thrill of saying, "See how wrong you are. I am the better parent." This was demonstrated when two parents argued at length about which of two available doctor's appointment times, 4 p.m. or 5 p.m., was in the best interests of their child. They both later said that they would have taken the child to an even earlier or later appointment if the doctor's office had offered only one time. Both thought they had to be right and both were very invested in proving it to each other. This sense of importance or investment in being right is a hint that the ego is involved. Try to think of an instance where conflict with your co-parent was resolved by one of you saying to the other, "Gee, you're right. I don't know why I didn't see it your way. My apologies." In our experience, that just does not happen in conflictual divorces. Trying to convince your co-parent that she is wrong and you are right generally does not work.

Holding On to Changing the Other

Here, each of you tries to change the other through criticism and lectures, as if there is a chance you will be successful in changing each other's viewpoint, behavior, or personality. "Why are you so self-absorbed?" "When will you put the children's needs above your own?" "You are such a liar." These are just a few of the judgmental, demeaning, and conflict-inducing comments that you say to one another. If you have been the recipient of such statements, have you ever found them helpful? Our bet is you have not said to yourself or the other person, "Gee, I appreciate that. I never noticed that about myself. I'm glad you pointed it out as it is something I should be working on." Similarly, the person you may have said such things to is not likely to change for the better because of your advice. This is especially true in divorce. If your co-parenting partner was going to change based on your attempts and comments, we would expect that would have occurred during the course of the marriage and not in the midst of conflict and confrontation.

Holding On to Justification

Parents in high-conflict divorces often feel justified in their positions. Each reacts to the other, saying in one way or another, "You can't do that to me. Why are you so difficult? Why are you so impossible?" The conflict escalates in a way that is similar to that of two children (or countries) who begin to argue, both justifying their actions of retaliation as legitimate responses to the perceived threats or attacks of the other. This cycle of *reciprocal retribution* leads to schoolyard fights and countries and families at war.

Holding On to Sharing Our Feelings

This is a controversial area. Many therapists and experts speak to the importance of sharing feelings. However, we often see this backfire when divorced parents use the sharing of feelings as a cover for blame and criticism, as in the comment, "I feel that you are a self-absorbed moron." This is not really a feeling (or a statement of one's emotion). Rather, it is a thought, judgment, opinion, or perception said in a hostile way and thinly disguised as a "feeling."

We also wonder what parents expect will happen by sharing their feelings with their co-parent. How will it lead to a productive resolution? Imagine calling customer service of a bank, airline, or store with a complaint and hearing the representative voice his feelings or emotional reaction to your complaint. At that moment, you are probably caring more about resolution than hearing the representative's feelings and assessment of your character. Likewise, how likely is it that the other parent is really going to respond positively to the feelings that you voice? Does he really care? Did he respond positively in the midst of the marriage?

Holding On to the Need for Respect

"You should treat me with respect." "Why should I respect you, after what you did to our marriage?" These are common statements made by co-parents who have a history of conflict. Let's look at what these kinds of comments do to the level of conflict and the underlying relationship. In the first comment you are making a demand of the other (*you* should treat me with respect), while in the second you are asking for justification (why should I respect *you?*). However, these two seemingly opposite comments are quite similar. In both statements, you are making your own behavior conditional on the other person's. That is, the first comment can be reworded or interpreted as "I will behave toward you differently only after you treat me with respect." The second comment is doing the same thing and can be interpreted as "I will behave toward you differently when you can justify or convince me that you're worth it." In both of these instances, the speaker is saying, "My behavior is based on yours." It is almost as if you are a sort of robot reacting to the actions of your co-parent, or at least that you will behave in a way that is conditional on what your co-parent does, whether it is helpful or healthy or child-focused, or not. Who is in control of you: you or your co-parent? Why give that control away to your co-parent?

Holding On to the Old Patterns of Defensive Communication

The cycles of conflict discussed above often involve an outward display of defensive communication. It can show up in the three different types of behaviors that we described in chapters 1 through 3 called fight, flight, or freeze behaviors. These behaviors may be very familiar and can be "left over" from the marital dynamics and interactions. They are not the behaviors that we would see in the business world if the corporation's values were to have world-class customer service. In a healthy business environment, communication problems and unmet expectations are not dealt with in hostile or aggressive ways. Rather, the issue is handled in a rational, businesslike fashion (see "Taking a World-Class Customer Service Approach" below for more on how to let go of defensive communication).

Now let's look at what you might be holding on to.

Exercise 5.4: Where's the Baggage?

In your journal, write about what you are holding on to. Is it the anger, the past, the truth, being right, changing your partner, justification, the need to share feelings, the need for respect, or old patterns of communication? Is it about something else? Next, write about whether the emotion or perception is providing something of use to you, or whether you'd be better off without it. When an issue arises, what other things could you focus on that just might work better for you? Make a list of them. They might come in very handy in the future to help you shift your attention off of the conflict and your emotional reaction.

Reducing Conflict

In addition to letting go of the common emotional causes of conflict, there are several alternatives to lessen the conflict. None of these are a panacea. None of them may be easy. None of them are going to change your parenting partner. However, we have found that each of these strategies may help *you* deal with the situation more effectively.

Quieting the Ego

There is an old Buddhist expression that says, "If you meet the ego, kill it." We certainly are not advocates for killing the ego. However, we think at times we need to gently say to the ego, "Not now. Go take a nap." Dealing with your co-parent is not where you should look for votes of confidence, enhancing your self-esteem, or getting respect and understanding. It is a time to do the business of parenting and simply to preserve yourself by not bringing your ego to the "party." In short, do not define interactions with your co-parent as being about you or your character.

Imagine telling your five-year-old he has to go to sleep before he's ready. He is overtired and cries out, "I hate you. You're a bad mommy." Do you take your child seriously? Do you think he really hates you? Do you believe that you are really a bad parent? Or, do you say to yourself "he is just reacting to the situation right now," but you know he doesn't hate you, even if he hates what is happening at the moment? In essence, you don't let your ego get activated by what your child says. Instead, you stay with your own concept of being a loving parent. Not taking what your child says about you as truth helps you respond more effectively at that moment.

Of course, it is more difficult in divorce when your former spouse, who likely has learned your emotional Achilles' heels, attacks the areas where you are most likely to have self-doubt and heightened reactions. However, imagine, when attacks come, saying to yourself something such as:

He is just upset and making a lot of noise.

He doesn't define me.

His opinion is his, but that doesn't make it right.

I am who I am and don't need his approval.

Of course he is upset. That is understandable. He usually gets upset at these sorts of things.

Changing how *you* deal with what your co-parent says is a more effective way of coping than trying to get your co-parent to change. You can be and feel more in control by managing your own response to your co-parent's behavior, rather than trying to manage your co-parent. When you manage your response, you can shield yourself from the impact of criticism.

Exercise 5.5: Insulating Myself Against Criticism

Think about one criticism from your co-parent that gets you upset or insults you. Now, think about what you know in your heart to be true about yourself as it relates to that comment. Which is more accurate—what your co-parent said, or what you know to be true?

The key here is to quiet the ego by *not accepting* what you know is not true about you, just like you would not accept as truth that your child thinks you're a bad parent. Instead, focus on what you know to be true about yourself, regardless of what your hostile "audience" says. If you hold on to what you know to be true about yourself, the comments of your co-parent (while annoying) cannot trigger your ego to go into a defensive mode.

Controlling Defensive Communication

In most parenting dialogues, you are both a speaker and receiver in the communication dynamic. We want to separate these two functions. As the speaker, you have lots of choice over what you say in response to a problem, need of your child, or comment from your co-parent. You can decide to make a hostile or negating comment (fight) or avoid commenting altogether (flight). Or, you can focus on *not* getting distracted by the opportunity to engage in conflict. That is, you can stay focused on the decision at hand and come up with a viable action plan.

Think about this hostile-sounding question:
"When are you ever going to sign our child up for the school trip?"
As the listener, you might say to yourself things such as:

Why can't I ever be appreciated for all I do for our child?

Why is she always so nasty to me? I don't deserve this attitude.

Why can't she sign our child up for the school trip? Why is it my job?

When you switch to the role of speaker, you might respond this way, especially if you have let your ego get involved:

"You're a parent; why don't you sign her up?"—Criticism

"When I feel like it."—Avoidance

"When you pay me your share for the last trip."—Linking

Defensive communication usually occurs when your ego has been triggered. Unfortunately, defensive communication is usually experienced as offensive by your co-parent, and it usually increases (rather than decreases) conflict. It is not really a good defense, as it does not protect you from the conflict and instead increases the very thing (the conflict) you are trying to avoid.

Exercise 5.6: Defending Myself Without Being Defensive

Let's reimagine this same situation about the trip, but with your ego taken out of it. Pretend that you know in your heart this is not at all about you. What can you tell yourself instead? See if you can construct an answer that simply addresses the problem of the child not being signed up for the trip. In other words, come up with an action plan. Try to not get distracted by the blame and nastiness of the question. You have nothing to prove or defend against. Imagine it just doesn't matter what your co-parent thinks. Instead, what matters is simply whether your child gets signed up for the trip. Does your child benefit in some way if your co-parent does it? Or, does your child benefit by it simply being done promptly and correctly? What would you say if you were not directly involved but were simply trying to make sure the child was signed up for the trip? Notice the difference in what you say from this perspective compared with our example of the critical, avoidant, and linking responses above.

Taking a World-Class Customer Service Approach

Great customer service departments are masters at avoiding defensive communication. The frustration, anger, or even insults of the customers do not entrap the representatives. Rather, they focus on acknowledging the feeling and taking an action to solve the problem. In our experience, the customer service representatives at L.L.Bean say, "We are sorry you are not 100% satisfied with the product. Send it back." If Starbucks gets the order wrong, the clerk apologizes and makes you a new cup of coffee. However, other companies blame the customer (for example, tell you that they made the coffee the way you told them to, tell you what their policy is and refuse to address your problem). Which one works better when you are on the receiving end?

Excellence in customer service is, among other things, about "wowing" the customer. You want them to say "Wow!" Imagine if your co-parent is about to ask you for some consideration or accommodation. Perhaps he is certain that you will refuse, give him a hard time, or ask for something in return. Imagine if you surprised him and simply said, "Sure. No problem." Whether he says it out loud or not, it is quite possible that he just said a "Wow!" These "wows" are not about liking or respecting the "customer." They are just done to try to build good will and avoid unnecessary conflict and the energy and time it takes to deal with it (sometimes parents argue over a fifteen-minute change in schedule for hours, over the course of days).

Think about how you enforce policies with your co-parent. Are you the "store" with the customer-friendly policy? Or, are you the one that makes transactions and doing business difficult? Businesses that have world-class customer service also train their personnel to avoid arguing with difficult customers. They do not quickly resort to calling security, but rather they address the difficult customer's needs as efficiently as possible and move on, rather than allowing that customer to influence other customers or take up a lot of staff time.

When we work with parents in high-conflict divorces, we see few examples of high-quality "customer service." Imagine, though, if you set the standard for quality co-parenting and reacting from a customer service perspective. By the way, the customer service representative on the other end of the call in the world-class company may not be feeling as pleasant as she sounds. She may have other issues she is contending with, or even perceive criticism or complaints in your tone or words. However, she "doesn't go there." Rather, she maintains an appropriate and positive attitude and focuses on addressing and solving the problem at hand.

Exercise 5.7: Providing Good Customer Service

In your journal, write down a recent situation that your co-parent complained about. Now, write down a well-crafted world-class customer service response to address the problem. Pretend that you are on the job and will go home after dealing with your difficult "customer." Pretend you and the customer don't even know each other. You are just there to solve the problem.

Does what you just wrote differ from how you actually responded to your co-parent? Even if you predict neither response would work to change your co-parent's response, which response do you feel better about? Which response helps you keep calm and centered?

Risking Vulnerability

I don't trust you. Why should I be vulnerable? These are common thoughts of parents in conflict. Yet in ancient times, warrior chieftains would often seek peace by going without weapons to speak to another chieftain. They would arrive with an open tunic to show they did not have weapons and to demonstrate an intention for peace. It is thought that the handshake evolved from such gestures. In high-conflict divorce, we often ask ourselves, *Why should I be vulnerable—again?* As long as you are unwilling to risk being vulnerable, you will likely be in an attack or defense mode. If you take the risk of being emotionally vulnerable, you just might be able to concentrate on improving your working relationship for the sake of your children.

An example of this occurred with one divorced couple in high conflict whose attorneys were not able to mediate a change in the parenting schedule long after the divorce. After about four or five mediation sessions, the mother, at the outset of an appointment, brought the father a small bag of his favorite snack food, saying, "I remembered that you like these and thought you might want some." He simply said, "Thank you." However, that was a turning point in their work. The "peace offering" and acceptance of the snack food made an impact that allowed them to progress, resolve the parenting plan dispute, and begin to work better together. The mother could have thought, *Why bother? He can buy his own snack. He's not going to appreciate it and will probably refuse it anyway.* And the father could have thought, *Why is she trying to manipulate me?* However, the gesture was intended and received as thoughtful—that made all the difference.

The first step is recognizing that the concept of true vulnerability may be misapplied when you as parents see *yourselves* as vulnerable. How are *you* going to get hurt by your co-parent's rage or nastiness? If that father refused the snack food, what does that really say about the mother? Or, does it say more about the father? If the mother can keep a rational perspective, she might not really see herself as being vulnerable; rather, she would notice that the father can be annoying and difficult to deal with but is not truly a threat. The real vulnerability to a conflictual parental relationship is not owned by you as parents, but rather by your children, as they are the ones most impacted by parents who are at "war."

Exercise 5.8: Decreasing My Vulnerability

In your journal, jot down how you presently are most vulnerable to your co-parent. Is this a physical or psychological risk? If it is a physical risk, what safeguards do you need to have in place? Please see the comments in the book's introduction about how to seek help if this is the case. If it is a psychological risk, what power are you giving your co-parent over your emotional well-being? Can you see how you are interpreting your co-parent's statements or behavior as having some degree of validity that influences your response? What if your co-parent's opinion was just that—his opinion? What does his opinion mean? What does his opinion mean about you? We think your co-parent's opinion does not define you in the slightest and that therefore you are not threatened or made vulnerable by it, even if it is annoying.

Setting the Standard

Making the decision to decrease the conflict can also help a parent decide to set the standard for excellence in co-parenting. Unfortunately, when conflict is the standard, parents tend to drop to the lowest level in the most important and difficult job of their lives—raising their children. Imagine if one or both of you set the standard for excellence in co-parenting, regardless of the behavior of your co-parent, perhaps saying to yourself, *I'm going to be the best co-parent I can possibly be, with or without your help.* That parent sets the standard of peace and appropriate communication. When that happens regularly, your children have at least one parent reaching for a higher standard. You can be the model. In some circumstances, your co-parent starts to "get it" and changes her behavior, especially if she realizes she does not have to defend herself because she is not being attacked. Either way, if you stop engaging in the conflict, you can focus your energy more on co-parenting and taking care of your children without being encumbered by fear, resentment, anger, and all the associated stress.

Exercise 5.9: Setting My Standards

Imagine your co-parenting relationship is a business that you jointly own. List your corporate policies related to your standards for the best co-parenting possible, regardless of whether your co-parent complies. What is your policy for communicating with your co-parent (regardless of how he acts)? How will you deal with complaints? How will you terminate an interaction? How much time will you let pass before responding? What are the policies and standards for your behavior (in other words, for your co-parenting customer service)? You can come back to this list, especially when your co-parent is being difficult, just as you would refer to your corporate policies when there is a difficult problem at work.

Triage: Here and Now

When you are in a high conflict dynamic with your co-parent, every situation can feel like an emergency. An important skill to develop is going into a "triage" mind-set, meaning that unless you've been called to the emergency room because one of your children has had an injury, sudden illness, or car accident, you are probably *not* dealing with a life-and-death crisis and don't have to react. Certainly, if you are dealing with a crisis, you must act thoughtfully and mindfully in a timely way. Even emergency responders don't run up to an accident scene; they walk with intention and, at the same time, care. In most situations, before acting, it is helpful to take a breath, pause, and tune in to your inner experience as well as the details of the external situation. You want to stay in control so that you can consider your options, think about the pros and cons of any particular action, and make thoughtful decisions.

One way to guide your thinking is to ask yourself, *How serious is this problem on a scale of 1 to 10, with 10 being a life-threatening emergency?* Are you escalating a small problem to a much larger one in your mind because your threshold for distress with your co-parent is so low and your tolerance is diminished?

Consider this scenario: Peter was transitioning his four children, ages six to fifteen, back to their mom's house after they had been with him on vacation for a week. As he was rounding up the children to leave his home, he realized at the last minute that he couldn't find his four-year-old daughter Maria's snow boots, the day before a storm was anticipated. They were nowhere to be found, and he felt pressed to get the children back. The children's things had gotten misplaced in his home before, and while he did not think it was a big problem, he knew that his co-parent, Dina, considered it a major catastrophe when something was missing. As a result, he avoided calling Dina to give her a heads-up about the missing boots and just sent Maria back to her house without them.

On Peter's part, this was an indication of his own difficulty tolerating distress. He chose to avoid Dina's reaction and his response to it. Predictably, Dina was extremely upset and reacted immediately and intensely. The children were in her emotional space and experienced her wrath. They (especially Maria) likely felt responsible for not being able to remember or find the boots.

Peter had dropped the children off and left the scene (flight), and was hostile to Dina (fight) when she called him in an uproar to complain. Peter, anticipating that Dina would be upset, had chosen not to alert her to the situation of the lost boots. This "surprise" then predictably led to Dina's increased distress and display of anger in front of the children, rather than just with Peter. If asked, Peter would probably say that in a truly life-threatening situation he would "take the hit" or step in front of the bus rather than let his children get hurt. Yet here, Peter did a "drop and run" to avoid Dina's reaction, which disrupted the children's return to her from their vacation with Dad.

Dina did not consider the magnitude of her response or the impact of it. A situation that might have been a 0.5 or a 1.0 in potential danger was escalated to a crisis. This hurt everyone. Dina was operating from a place of refusing to accept the reality of her life. She did not recognize her choice to focus on the frustration and distress rather than the joy and experience of her children returning home. She did not choose to use a triage mindset and put aside the issue of the lost boots and Peter's failure to disclose that they were missing. She did not recognize Peter's repeated problems with disorganization and time pressure, and perhaps some of his shame and embarrassment, and consequently his avoidance of an anticipated barrage. Instead, she saw it as another sign that he is an incompetent father and a terrible person who ruined her life and the lives of her children and their return to her after a week away.

Did Peter ruin the transition back to Mom's? Did Dina ruin it? Or, might you say they both played a part in how the transition went? And, who were they focusing on? Each other. They were not focusing on the experience of the children and asking, "How do we make this transition (the end of the vacation with Dad and their return to Mom) as easy and positive as possible for the children?"

Instead, Peter could have texted an apology in advance before leaving for Dina's. He could have also told her he would look for the boots later and if he did not find them would pick up another pair for Maria and bring them to her. Dina could have said in response, "I understand. No problem." She also could say that she has other boots that will fit Maria and that Peter could just bring the boots to her when they turn up. Dina then could have looked out the window eagerly awaiting the return of the children (boots or no boots) to greet them with love and joy.

If Dina were practicing distress tolerance (see below), she might have been able to experience her initial reaction of frustration and distress and take a deep breath, reassigning the level of distress and refocusing on the most important part of the children's return—all of them reconnecting with her after a week. Recognizing that these things can throw her into her monkey-brain self, she might have taken out her distress-tolerance first aid kit and chosen one or more of the tools to soothe herself and let her reasonable mind begin to problem solve. Let's take a look at some of the basic ingredients of a distress-tolerance kit.

Distress-Tolerance First Aid

You can put more items in the kit if you'd like, but we think at a minimum you should have the following five items or strategies for dealing with your immediate reaction to stress. Notice that none of the items below relate to changing your co-parent. They address your concentration, body, and mind.

Focus on Your Breath

As we discussed in chapter 3, focusing on breathing has been done across the centuries and across many cultures to help quiet the mind and calm the body. Your breath is always with you. When stressed, you can simply focus on slowing and deepening your breathing. Even with your eyes open, you can concentrate on your breathing, centering and calming your nervous system *before* you react to your co-parent, or your children.

Do Some Cardio Exercise

Increasing your heart rate can go a long way to helping counteract the stress response. Exercise boosts your endorphins (the chemicals that make you feel good) and can help take your focus off the stress. It can shift you from the stress response into a calmer place, which can then help you react more effectively to the stress.

Cold Water

When you're having an argument with your co-parent, do you feel flushed? Do your ears feel hot? Are you "hot under the collar"? These are natural responses to being angry and upset. It can take a while for these physical sensations to subside on their own. You can hasten the process by using cold water. Washing your face with ice-cold water can help you "chill down" and reorient you away from the agitated, angry, stressed response, restoring your normal equilibrium.

Calming Statements

In chapter 3, we discussed the use of self-statements. Certainly, these belong in your distress-tolerance first aid kit. You can have key statements on a card that you can read when needed. While it may seem a little hokey or contrived, these statements can serve as a mantra for dealing with the times you get activated. For example, writing down statements such as "My co-parent's view of me is not me" and "I'm the person and parent I am regardless of his feelings toward me " can help remind you of what you know to be true. You can also use simple calming reminders, along with your breathing, by slowly repeating the word *calm* or *relax* to yourself as you inhale and exhale.

Focus on Practical Solutions

Focusing on practical solutions can get you away from spinning your wheels thinking about why your co-parent said or did what he did. Practical solutions can help you get a clear perspective about the matter at hand. Just like the pilot who focuses on what needs to be done to land the plane safely in an emergency (rather than what could have prevented the emergency), when you are in the midst of a stressful situation, you too can focus on what needs to be done (in a very practical way) to address the problem as it relates to the children.

Some people find it helpful to keep their distress-tolerance first aid kit close at hand. It's like putting a typical first aid kit in the back of your car or in your backpack. In the case of your distress-tolerance first aid kit, you can list the steps or prompts that work for you on a card and keep it in your wallet or cell phone case. When you're stressed, you can go to it and use what you think would be most helpful to quiet your mind and body. Once you calm the mind and stop the rush of fight, flight, or freeze chemicals through your body, you can engage in problem solving to assess what needs to be done to deal with the situation with the children's best interests in mind.

Recovery

It is freeing to embrace the idea that the only person you can save is yourself. You cannot change your co-parent. When you focus your energy on your own healing and recovery, you can shift from seeing yourself as a victim to becoming your own hero (as we discussed in chapter 4). Participating in your own recovery includes taking care of your physical self with rest, relaxation, good nutrition, and exercise. In addition, knowing which people in your life are true friends and supports, and which people create drama or negativity in your life, can help a lot. Pay attention to nurturing the relationships that nurture you and enhance your feeling of well-being. Similarly, letting go of relationships that are not supportive and nurturing and are full of "drama" can also bring a level of calmness into your world.

Your recovery may also include a plan for your future. If you are working, assessing whether your work gives you a feeling of purpose and value is important. You can also assess whether it is providing enough money to give you a basic sense of financial security. What else do you need to meet your future goals?

Finally, your recovery involves fully grieving your loss and moving forward into your future. You may wish to engage a therapist, join a support group, or connect with a close group of friends to heal most fully. When you find yourself going back into the past, or wishing things were different, or raging at your co-parent (in reality or in your mind), you need to catch yourself, hit the reset button, and think about one small self-nurturing goal you can set for yourself each day that supports your recovery. Ask yourself, "What constitutes a healthy and authentic life for me?"

Radical Acceptance

One key concept here is learning to practice *radical acceptance*, which means being willing to accept ourselves as we are and our lives as they are (Brach 2003). In a sense, it is like the serenity prayer used in Alcoholics Anonymous and other 12-step programs: "God grant me the serenity to accept the things I cannot change; courage to change the things I can; and wisdom to know the difference." Such acceptance helps us avoid the frustration of trying to change what we cannot change (like your co-parent's attitude and personality). It helps you avoid the struggle of fighting a hopeless battle. It is the difference between fretting when getting caught in a huge downpour and focusing on getting to your destination (even though you are soaking wet). Radical acceptance can help you avoid spending precious energy on what cannot be changed. It can also help you avoid reacting without thought and causing new problems and then bitterness from the original ones (like panicking in the downpour, taking off running, and then slipping in the mud).

Using Your First Aid Kit

Let's now put it all together. In sports and the performing arts they call it building *muscle memory* as you imagine and rehearse using the skills over and over until they are second nature. Here we can help you work on your emotional muscle memory, especially for dealing with some common situations that you face.

Exercise 5.10: Building "Muscle Memory"

List some stressful and conflictual situations that seem to occur over and over with your co-parent. Perhaps they relate to transitions, changing the schedule, or parenting policies. Next, rather than analyzing your co-parent's behavior, look at your own reactions. Go back through this chapter and look at the different skills and approaches we've discussed. Then list which approaches might help you respond or react differently. Don't think about what will lead to a successful outcome on the issue. Rather, think about what you need to do in order to deal with your co-parent's predictable behavior without getting yourself tied in knots or drawn into the conflict. What do you need to react to? What do you need to let go? How do you want to use your voice? What self-statements do you need to make to stay calm? What do you need to do to recover emotionally if you get activated? Put together a plan that is specific to each situation. Then, imagine yourself following through on the plan. Imagine this over and over again, and imagine feeling more in control and more centered, regardless of your co-parent's reaction. Then, try to use this plan when situations arise. Don't expect to be perfect. Just start to rely more and more often on what can help you be in charge of your own reactions.

Wrapping It Up

In this chapter, we focused on the ego's role in conflict as well as options to quiet the ego, that is, to develop a healthier view of your self. Using this skill in everyday situations with your co-parent will help you to avoid personalizing your co-parent's actions or words. Understanding the three cycles of conflict—downward spiral, negative intimacy, and linking—helps you to recognize how your emotions get triggered and put into practice various ways of containing the conflict. Incorporating a triage mindset in challenging situations can help you keep things in perspective, and supplying your own distress-tolerance first aid kit will allow you to be at the ready when conflict arises. As you focus on applying the concepts in this and preceding chapters to your own situation with your co-parent, you will be able to begin to reduce the conflict and its impact on you and your children.

Taking It Home and Making It Yours

❋ Keep your ego out of interactions with your co-parent. Your co-parent's thoughts and feelings about you do not define you or your worth.

❋ Control your tendency to react emotionally or engage in the conflict. Once you're caught up in it, you lose your centeredness.

❋ Avoid defensive communication.

❋ Stay in the here and now and focus on addressing the practical issue at hand rather than debating logic, principles, and your co-parent's version of history.

❋ Build and use your distress-tolerance first aid kit.

❋ Practice radical acceptance—accepting yourself and your life as it is.

CHAPTER 6

Creating Safety in Co-parenting

In this chapter, we will discuss the importance of creating safe emotional attachments for your children to each of you, and a safe attachment to each other in your co-parenting relationship. We will look at the impact of different patterns of communication and how these patterns can either hurt or help your children. We will show you how to redefine your roles and make your emotionally hostile relationship more of a business relationship (that is, about the business of raising children). Most importantly, we will look at ways to stop these repetitive patterns, even if your co-parent is not motivated to do so.

Creating Safe Attachment

When we think of attachment, we often think of newborn infants and the process of bonding with their parents. This plays an influential role in their development and capacity to form other relationships and "connect" with those around them.

Once thought to be learned behavior, attachment is now widely understood to be hardwired in our DNA to ensure survival. One of your earliest tasks as parents is to foster secure attachment in your infants. Newborns' behaviors such as crying, smiling, and crawling are seen as ways of ensuring that their parents will stay close by and will be there to take care of them. John Bowlby (1969) described this evolutionary theory of attachment and the idea that insecurity and fear arise when infants are separated from their primary attachment figures—usually their parents. Infants can attach to multiple people, but social interactions and responsiveness are necessary for secure attachments to develop. As parents, you need to create a foundation of secure attachment by effectively responding to your children's needs, no matter their age. When divorce occurs, it becomes even more critical to pay attention to your children's need for secure attachment. The fulfillment of those needs should be at the forefront of your thinking and planning.

Attachment Theory Applied to Adult Love Relationships

Johnson and Sims (2000) describe how attachment is manifested in adult relationships. They discuss different styles of attachment, which can be healthy and loving or dysfunctional. Two patterns they describe seem particularly pertinent when it comes to looking at parental conflict. First, in *anxious attachment*, the connection between you and your partner may shift between being intensely positive and being hostile. You may be demanding and critical of your partner, and you may use emotional blackmail and engage your partner through hostile and dependent means. Second, in the pattern of *avoidant attachment*, you may not feel the need for emotional closeness and may marginalize or dismiss your partner's feelings. You may even avoid intimate relationships, saying that you just don't need closeness or that relationships just hurt people anyway. Shortly, we'll explore how these patterns may play a role in your postdivorce conflict.

Sue Johnson (2008) and others have also begun to recognize the importance of attachment theory in adult love relationships. The idea that your survival is based on bonding with a trusted partner, and that this is a compelling drive that is hardwired into your adult brain, is gaining more and more attention. The adult bond of attachment is defined by emotional accessibility, responsiveness, and engagement (Johnson 2008). When the attachment is secure, it can help you develop in a healthy way and maintain a sense of self that allows you to emotionally connect to others more easily. When you have a strong loving connection with a significant other, you can operate from a secure base and take more risks, knowing that you have a safe haven to return to. When you know that your partner is there for you and "has your back," you are more able to explore the world independently and be curious about yourself internally. Both your inner and outer world feel safer to approach with openness and curiosity.

Conversely, when this sense of connection with your partner is lost, the experience can be one of emotional isolation, pain, helplessness, and panic. When your attachment is not secure, your emotional growth can be stifled. You may approach your connections as either anxious and preoccupied or dismissive and avoidant. When you're anxiously attached, your nervous system is on high alert, searching for cues of rejection and abandonment. This is when you are most vulnerable to fight, flight, or freeze reactions. If you come into a relationship with an anxious attachment, you may find you're often needing intense connection for reassurance. Sometimes this means running headlong into a relationship and creating a lot of intensity at the start, an intensity that inevitably drops off as the relationship matures. You may also notice that when your partner tries to reassure you, you find it very difficult to trust that reassurance. Alternatively, when you come into a relationship with a personal history of avoidance and fear of attachment, you are likely to experience avoidant attachment in the relationship. You are probably expecting to be rejected at every turn, and you may become numb, shut down, and reject the support of others. Adults who enter relationships with a legacy of insecure attachment from their childhoods, whether anxious or avoidant attachment, have difficulty feeling that they're bonded with someone who makes them feel special and irreplaceable.

Exercise 6.1: My Attachment Assessment

This is a chance to go back and look at your own attachment history. First, think about your own experiences as a child with your parents (and maybe other important adults). Write in your journal about who comforted you when you were sad, hurt, or frightened. Were your parents trusted attachment figures? How was your bond with one parent different from the one you had with your other parent? Who did you turn to? How did that person make you feel? Were there other trusted attachment figures in your childhood? Describe them. Would you describe yourself as having been securely or insecurely attached, and if the latter, do you see the attachments as having been more anxious or more avoidant? Write about how your early experience with attachment influenced your adult relationships, your trust, your running to or away from relationships, and your experiences of hurt and betrayal. Write about how this might impact your current relationship with your co-parent. See what connections you can make between your past attachment issues and the conflict with your co-parent.

Adult Attachment Theory Applied to Parents in High Conflict

When a marriage ends, the relationship between spouses often feels unsafe. Yet, at the same time, as caregivers, it is important that you have the best working relationship possible. Your most powerful and protective role as parents is called into play here. We believe the real work of co-parenting needs to be about turning the bond as parents into one that is secure and functional, even though the bond as spouses has suffered mortal wounds. Each of you as parents should know that you are a valued member of this very small and crucially important team—the team of parents of the children you created.

A place to begin is to take a hard look at the current reality in your parenting team. Do you feel safe and secure knowing that your children have two parents who are aligned and committed to *working together* to create a safe emotional environment to nurture your children's growth? If your relationship with your co-parent is highly conflictual, then most likely the answer to this question is no. It can be helpful to first look at yourself and think about what you are doing that fosters or interferes with the bond between you as parents. Are you (as discussed in chapter 5) holding on to justification, anger, the past, your "truth," being right, changing the other, or old patterns of defensive communications that are interfering with creating the secure attachment in the parental bond that will ultimately support your children's well-being?

If you find yourself answering yes to these questions, it's important to begin working on your own side of the equation. Did you and your co-parent ever create a secure parental bond for your children? Did you come into the marriage with the capacity to securely attach to your partner? Are you capable of secure attachment? Was your partner capable of secure attachment? Have you completed an emotional divorce from your parenting partner? What are the psychological bruises from your childhood that have gotten in the way of this? What do you need to do to heal them?

These are not easy questions. They require you to honestly look at yourself as well as your partner. Be careful here; we do not want you to shift into viewing this as being about blame or guilt or negative self-judgment. Instead, it is about realistically seeing where you might need to focus, given the challenges that are present—challenges that in all likelihood you and your co-parent came to naturally by virtue of each of your own individual childhood and early adulthood experiences.

Stopping the Dysfunctional Patterns

Reviewing the breakdowns in communication presents unique opportunities for creating a roadmap to help you shift away from the dysfunctional patterns of interactions that occur with your co-parent. These repetitive patterns of behavior can come from the cycles we mentioned in chapter 5 (downward spiral, negative intimacy, linking). They can also come from repeated behaviors or habits of acting and communicating with one another in ways that lead to the relationship not feeling safe for one or both of you. From this roadmap of dysfunctional patterns, you can develop language that describes them and helps you identify and shift to healthier patterns, earlier and earlier in the process.

Exercise 6.2: Analyzing My Patterns with My Co-parent

In your journal, please describe a conflictual pattern that you and your co-parent often go through. Describe the features of it that happen repeatedly. What do you do? What does your co-parent do? How do things go amiss? How do one or both of you feel unsafe in the interaction? Now try to address a difficult question: what could you have done differently to avoid the problem or recover quickly as parenting partners? Write down as many options as possible. Especially focus on what *you* could do, even if your co-parent is not willing to change. You can try to experiment with these options, as you might try to experiment with adding different ingredients into a recipe.

Aligning Against the Patterns

These repetitive behaviors are predictable. By learning to recognize them and develop a language to identify them when they are happening in the moment, you can begin to gain some control over them. If you can develop a safe and strong bond with your co-parenting partner around your forever connection as parents of the children you created together, you can begin to deal with moments that trigger either one of you.

It is important to recognize your co-parent's need for validation of importance in the lives of your children. He or she is the most important parenting partner you have with these children (even if you are remarried to a terrific stepparent). This is a very important concept. Most co-parents get easily triggered when their importance is minimized, especially if this is done by the other parent. And in our experience, most co-parents do not openly and sincerely validate the importance of their co-parenting partner. Imagine if it were the other way around, and one or both co-parents understood that the role they play in the lives of their children is truly valued by the other parent. When both co-parents believe the other sees their importance, it generally is easier to work together to identify and shift the patterns.

Once you can see the pattern between you and identify it, you can focus on the big picture and not get sidetracked by the details. Sue Johnson (2008) describes cycles between couples in intimate relationships and calls them "demon dialogues." These take place when you are not able to connect to your partner in an emotionally safe way. We often see the patterns that began during the marriage continuing into the postdivorce co-parenting relationship. This ongoing negative pattern of interaction decreases your emotional safety as parents and consequently impacts your children. By not working together as parents, you have difficulty creating the protective container that your children need.

Johnson (2008) describes three basic cycles, or "dances," that exist in insecurely attached relationships. We often see these same three patterns in postdivorce parenting relationships. She calls the first "find the bad guy." In the postdivorce parenting relationship, we'd call this pattern "shaming and blaming." This is a pattern of mutual blame that keeps you distant and unable to focus on your children's needs because you are so busy focusing on each other's faults and inadequacies—as a parent or as a person. Reducing the blameful communication can help decrease the strength or power of this cycle and allow you to simply focus on the child-centered decisions that need to made at that moment.

Johnson (2008) calls the second dance the "protest polka." In postdivorce parenting, we would call it "knock, knock—hide and seek." In this pattern, one parent is constantly seeking out and criticizing the other, while the other parent is in defense mode and not interacting or fully responding to the issue at hand. Again, staying focused on the child-centered concerns (rather than engaging in criticism or defense) can help.

The third pattern, which Sue Johnson (2008) calls "freeze and flee," is one of hopelessness, when both parents withdraw from the parenting relationship and you are left with only numbness and distance in your connection around parenting your children. In these parental relationships, you are likely to retreat to what is called *parallel parenting*, with little attempt to communicate or work together. However, even if you find yourself in this pattern, you don't have to continue working in parallel. It can send a very positive message if you often give your co-parent plenty of information about the children and repeatedly include him in decisions (even if you can easily make these decisions on your own). The point here is to start to work together for the sake of the children (instead of maintaining the status quo of being two separate parenting systems that are not coordinated).

Your patterns may or may not be similar to those described by Johnson. If they're different, that's fine. The important point is to see the repeated patterns of interaction that don't work. Here's an example of a shaming and blaming pattern in action.

The Weekend from Hell

Charlie and Amanda's legal divorce has been final for over a year. They work hard to be the best parents they can be for their two children (Mike, age eight, and Emily, age twelve). Often, their plans to be their best selves are interrupted by hurt and anger that spill over from the past.

Last Friday, Charlie sent a note to Amanda letting her know that his girlfriend, Jackie, would be coming to Mike's lacrosse game on Sunday and expressing the wish that all the adults could stand together with the other parents and watch the game, cheering Mike on. Amanda agreed and set out to the lacrosse game with that expectation, only to find Charlie and Jackie standing by themselves on the other side of the field away from all the cheering parents. Amanda was surprised and taken aback. It was hard enough for her to have Charlie's girlfriend front and center in her community and at her son's game, but she couldn't figure out how the heads-up and invitation to stand together had ended up looking like this.

When trying to understand what prompted Charlie and Jackie to stand alone watching the game, we came to learn that earlier in the weekend, there had been a breakdown between Charlie, Amanda, and Jackie, and their choice of position on the field was an attempt to avoid conflict and "a scene" at the game. What had happened the previous day

*was a cascade of smaller breakdowns that ended in a heated debacle
with all of the grownups yelling at each other and the children watching
in horror. It began with Charlie helping out on Amanda's weekend by
taking their daughter Emily to a friend's birthday party. Amanda had
asked that he arrive an hour before the party to leave time for Emily to go
to the library to pick up a book. Charlie texted that rather than coming
an hour in advance, he would come fifteen minutes in advance.
Ultimately, he came only five minutes before the beginning of the party,
causing Emily to arrive late. Amanda insisted that they leave
immediately so they wouldn't be even later, and Jackie was insisting that
she first be dropped off at Charlie's house before they go to the party. The
adults were heading into a tailspin and the children were witnesses.*

*This rupture was not followed with repair. After the breakdown,
there was no further communication about how the adults would regroup
for the game on Sunday. Amanda assumed they would stand together as
planned, and Charlie and Jackie decided it was too risky. One
breakdown followed another, and the ultimate outcome was that when
Mike stood on the lacrosse field, he had to look on one side to see his
mom, and then turn the other way to see his dad and Jackie standing
alone, apart from all the other parents. What message did this send to
Mike? Here, the lack of parental communication and repair following the
incident on Saturday carried over to the lacrosse game on Sunday,
signaling to the children parental conflict and an inability for their
parents to work together.*

*What can we learn from analyzing the breakdown with Amanda
and Charlie? Let's look at the repeating pattern in the way they interact.
When Amanda asked Charlie to help out by taking over a parenting task
on her parenting time, she wanted to manage the logistics according to
her own sense of the time it takes to meet the children's needs, get them
moving, and travel to the locations they needed to get to. Charlie wanted
to manage the logistics himself according to his own sense of time and
was resentful of what felt like his being controlled or micromanaged by
Amanda. Charlie had a more easygoing sense of time and was not so
concerned about being five or ten minutes late. Amanda was anxious as
it became obvious to her that Charlie was cutting it close and was likely*

to be late. Jackie added her needs into the mix. She indicated that her need to return home was more important than Emily's need to be on time for the party. This further upset Amanda, who also interpreted the lateness as one more example of Charlie's overall incompetence as a parent and lack of caring for the children and prioritizing their needs (shaming and blaming him). That ruffled Charlie's feathers, as he saw himself as being a good dad and doing Amanda a favor by taking care of a child-related errand for her on her parenting time so she could take care of their other child.

After the meltdown they had in Amanda's driveway on Saturday, Charlie and Jackie felt shame about it. They unilaterally decided that they would keep their distance to avoid any other conflict on Sunday, and they did not communicate this decision to Amanda (to avoid the blame they anticipated from her). Amanda then felt blindsided on Sunday, continuing to go by the last communication she had with Charlie about standing together. In a sense, both parents felt shame about what happened and, in their own uncoordinated way, tried to address it (Charlie by standing on the other side trying to avoid a repeat performance, and Amanda following the original plan to try to behave in a more "normal" manner).

Charlie and Amanda had gotten stuck in a dangerous downward spiral that then eroded communication. The pattern of Amanda looking for Charlie's validation of her as an important co-parent was something that was being repeated. Amanda was again hurt and felt disregarded by what felt like the substitution of Charlie's girlfriend as a partner and parent. In other words, Amanda was not feeling safe and respected in her role as a co-parent. She also felt that Charlie was letting their children down by not prioritizing their needs over Jackie's needs. Her pattern of responding was to react to these feelings by being critical and harsh and protesting Charlie's ideas loudly. Charlie became worried about being called out by Amanda and being told he was "doing the wrong thing." He chose to take the route that seemed to provide the least opportunity for conflict, and stepped away. He might have been using the "when in doubt, say or do nothing" approach, which generally further impairs parental communication and creates more misunderstandings.

If Charlie and Amanda could have had a difficult conversation following the argument on Saturday where both acknowledged their own role in the breakdown, they may have been able to repair the rupture and together more consciously choose the best way to approach choreographing their time at Sunday's lacrosse game. Once again, their children would be watching intently. Seeing that a rupture between their parents could be repaired would have been very comforting for Emily and Mike. If two parents both commit to understanding the cycle, they can form a healthier container for the conflict so that it does not impact the children. And, even more so, they can show the children that recovery and healing is possible.

While Charlie and Amanda's pattern was one of shame and blame, there are, as you know, many other patterns that can occur between parents. Recognizing and understanding yours is an important step in being able to change them.

Familiar Refrains of High-Conflict Parents

Below are some common refrains of parents in conflict. See if any of these sound familiar to you.

- You should be punished for what you did.

- You don't deserve time with the kids.

- You're not as competent as I am.

- I'll never forgive you.

- It's your responsibility.

- I'm going to keep you guessing.

- I'll tell you one thing and then do something else (also known as a bait and switch).

- I'm not going to commit.

Exercise 6.3: Summarizing Our Co-parenting Patterns

See if you can summarize the patterns that take over your parenting relationship and threaten to hurt your children by filling in the blanks in the following statements. Then, based on all of your statements, write a paragraph that sums up your co-parenting relationship. If it's possible, share it with your co-parent. If not, use it as a way of becoming more mindful about your own contribution to the cycle and commit yourself to learning new options for your own responses. Be concrete and specific (not general or abstract) and do not engage in disguised blaming.

- The more I try to _____, the more you criticize and blame me, and then the more I get hurt and angry and push your buttons, and round and round we go.

- When _____, I do not feel safely connected to you. (Write down the trigger that starts up the feeling of being disconnected.)

- I tend to _____. I move this way in our patterns of conflict to try to cope with difficult feelings and find a way to change them. (Choose an action word, such as complain, nag, zone out, ignore you, run, move away.)

- I do it in the hope that _____. (State the hope that pulls you into the pattern, such as "We will avoid more conflict" or "I will persuade you to respond to me more" or "I will persuade you to do the right thing by our children.")

- As this cycle keeps going, I feel _____. (Identify a feeling. The usual ones that people can identify at this point are frustration, anger, numbness, pain, hurt, emptiness, or confusion.)

- What I then say to myself about our parenting relationship is _____. (Summarize the most catastrophic conclusion you reach, such as "You do not care about me or our children; I am not important to you; the children are not important to you.")

- My understanding of the circular cycle of conflict that makes it harder and harder for us to safely connect is that when I move in the way I described above, you seem to then _____. (Choose a phrase with an action word, a verb, such as shut down, criticize me in the harshest words you can find, pressure me to respond.)

- The more I _____, the more you _____. We are then both trapped in pain and isolation. (Insert verbs that describe your own and your co-parent's moves in the cycle of conflict.)

- Maybe we can warn each other when this cycle begins. We can call it _____. Seeing this cycle is our first step out of the circle of disconnection that cripples us as parents.

Once you can identify these negative patterns or cycles and recognize that they trap both of you, you are ready to learn how to step out of them.

Stopping the Pattern

Once you've identified the dysfunctional pattern in your co-parenting, you can begin to dismantle it using these five steps:

1. Recognize the pattern. When you find things beginning to unravel with your co-parent, step back and call it as it is, saying, "We are doing the same old thing with one another again. Can we talk about this differently?" If your co-parent is unable to engage in this conversation, you are still in a position to say to yourself, *We're caught up in a breakdown and we're both getting hurt and hurting our kids. I need to shift out of doing what doesn't work and try a different way of responding. I need to use my first aid kit.*

2. Tell yourself, *Here we go again. What am I doing to stay trapped in this pattern, and how am I trapping my co-parent?* If you're attacking your co-parent, you're putting him on the defense, creating a need for him to justify his behavior and making it hard for him to be open and responsive to you. If you withdraw and stay apart, you're pulling your co-parent into pursuing you and pushing for communication and connection (you could call this pattern "push me—pull you").

3. Recognize that the underlying problem here is that both of you have created an unstable and unsafe parenting connection. We have found that simple communication and problem-solving techniques need to be combined to address the problem at hand in a practical way. You don't have to agree on the history, who is to blame, who is right, or who has the more accurate understanding of the issue at hand. At the same time, clearly reaffirming your co-parent's value and importance and recommitting to work together can help stabilize the connection.

4. See the unhealthy pattern of responding (not your co-parent) as the enemy of your stable co-parenting and your children's safe emotional world.

5. Strive to learn to call the pattern by name. You can use a name as a kind of shorthand that makes sense to you (and possibly

your co-parent). Then, slow the dialogue down and create enough safety to speak honestly about the behaviors that are more respectful and can help build a new pattern of communicating and decision making.

As you can see, all of these steps involve looking at your own contributions to the unhealthy interactions. Most people spend far more energy looking at and talking to others about their co-parent's reactions and unreasonableness, but this does little to make a positive difference when the only person you can possibly have control over is yourself.

Exercise 6.4: Looking at My Own Contributions

Think of an incident with your co-parent where you fell into the same old pattern of conflict. Write down the explanations you used to try to win the fight or prove your innocence. Did you accuse your co-parent of making a mess of things? What were your usual comebacks when you felt cornered? What did you say or do (or not say or do) to provoke your co-parent? Then, sketch out the patterns of hostile criticism and labeling that traps you both and hurts your children. How did each of you begin to define the other? How did each of you wound and enrage the other? Now, try to rewrite this, only focusing on your behavior. If you could do it all over again, what would you have done differently? Whether it changed the actual outcome or not, what feelings would be different for you if you had responded differently? List these in your first aid kit as well. These are the behaviors to experiment with the next time you are dealing with your co-parent around a challenging issue. Repeatedly try these and other alternatives. Notice how you feel when you do so. Are you hurt and enraged, or more centered and in control?

When Your Co-parent Isn't a Partner in Stopping the Conflict

If you begin to recognize recurrent breakdowns with your co-parent, and she is not interested in exploring these with you, does that leave you stuck in endless conflict? Not if you are willing to explore your own role and take serious measures to change your reactions. One parent can start to change the average level of conflict. You can be the parent who sets the stage for change. You can take the high road and be the best co-parenting partner, even if your co-parent is not doing so. In this instance, the children at least have one parent communicating effectively. There is a chance that if you are this parent, after a time, your co-parent might just start to slowly improve her behavior, not even knowing why or what is different. She might even later take all the credit for the change. This is fine. Just as you don't need the blame, you also don't have to take the credit for the positive change that occurs.

Redefining Your Roles

Either one of you can make it your priority to shift away from the identity of warring ex-spouses and focus on the work of co-parenting. You do not have to match your co-parent's poor judgment, choices, or parental behavior. When it comes to something about your children, you can always strive to take the high road.

Using a Business Model

If you begin to see yourself and your co-parent as operating in a business model (as we discussed in chapter 5) and start treating each other as the co-CEOs and board of directors of your children's lives, you can begin to decrease the opportunities for negative patterns to flourish and recur. Co-CEOs and directors on a board don't always *agree*. Rather, they *decide, following a process* (even if the vote is 51% to 49%). As parents, you don't have the luxury of having an odd number of people to make the decision. That means that at times you have to accommodate the other, meet in the middle, or figure out a solution that respects both of the different points of views and addresses your co-parent's concerns as well as your own. When you are trying to sustain a functional partnership and a flourishing business, you need to (1) stick to the problems and options for problem solving, (2) maintain clear communication that is limited to dealing with the issues at hand, and (3) honor your agreements and routinely follow through on them. Similarly, not getting into senseless conflict with your most important business partner—your-co-parent—is key.

While we often refer to co-parenting as a "business relationship," your children are more important than a business. They are precious people you created and have invested heavily in, who you certainly want to grow and thrive. Business partners do not have to like one another. Businesses don't always trust their customers (and vice-versa). Yet business is done best by offering excellence in customer service (as discussed in chapter 5) and delivering on what you promise. How does this apply to co-parenting?

Imagine if you could calculate how many hours per week you are engaged with your co-parent over trivial details. What if you accommodated your co-parent on many of these? How much would it matter in the long run to the well-being of your children? What would your co-parent get and how would it benefit you if the battles were avoided? What happens when you seek an accommodation? Do you get immediate push-back and resistance? Do you offer an even exchange (for instance, when you want to shift days) and then get surprised that it is not immediately accepted? Sometimes these offers are actually not experienced as "even" or "fair" because they may inconvenience your co-parent or not work in his schedule. We have seen parents actually offer more than an even exchange as they look for a scheduling accommodation. For example, a parent wanting a few extra days with the children on the December holiday break offered the other parent a week more vacation time over the summer. Instead of no, she heard "Really? That would be great!" In other words, if this were a retail business, she "wowed" the customer by offering a discount *and* paying for the shipping and the return if needed.

Exercise 6.5: Wowing My Co-parent

List some ways you can "wow" your co-parent. Perhaps create a menu of things you can offer that just might be appreciated by your co-parent. Whenever you think of it, add it to the list. Then when needed, go back to the list before you ask for an accommodation. Next, list some ways you can "wow" your co-parent when he is looking for an accommodation. For example, imagine if your co-parent asked, "Can I bring the kids back a half-hour later?" Might your co-parent experience a "wow" if you said in response, "A half hour? Do you need more time than that? If so, just let me know what you need." It is pretty hard for your co-parent to engage in conflict when he experiences a "wow."

Bringing on a Consultant

Sometimes a consultant can help in your co-parenting, just as it can help in business. A consultant can help you focus on your mission and vision and define the steps needed to move forward. When it comes to divorce, there are few different types of consultants. *Co-parent counselors* concentrate on helping you communicate, plan, make decisions as parents, and decrease the conflict between you. *Parenting coordinators* can help get you out of the conflict by assisting you in arriving at decisions when you are at an impasse. Sometimes parenting coordinators are authorized to make binding recommendations to parents, especially when conflict tends to impede important decision making. Your own individual therapist can also be an important consultant if you focus some of your time with your therapist on how to avoid contaminating your co-parenting relationship when you feel provoked.

Paying Attention to Your Co-parent's Strengths

In the midst of high-conflict postdivorce parenting, it is easy to get lost in the attacks (that come to you, and the ones you initiate). This certainly limits the ability to create a sense of safe attachment as parents. Yet, besides all the flaws that surfaced during and after your divorce, you each have strengths. While you may be aware of your strengths, it can be harder (through all the attacks) to communicate your appreciation of *your co-parent's* strengths.

What can often be most helpful is for you to clearly acknowledge the importance and value of your co-parent. You can focus on being responsive and dependable around parenting issues, creating a sense that you are part of a partnership for the benefit of your children. You can also explicitly recognize and reinforce your co-parent's strengths.

Exercise 6.6: My Co-parent's Strengths

Take a moment and think of your children's experience with their other parent. What does your co-parent contribute to your children's well-being? List any positive attributes of your co-parent when it comes to the children. This can be your go-to list when you need to get out of the conflict and want to move toward a more positive dialogue. You can also keep these positive attributes in mind when you are trying to make plans with the other parent so that you are planning in a way that aligns with your co-parent's strengths. Focusing on your co-parent's strengths can increase the positive interactions between you both.

Using Structure and Technology as Tools for Best Practices

We have found that the use of available tools can help parents stay focused, contain conflict, and begin to build the parental team that will support their children. However, these tools do not have to be very complicated or costly. Generally, a lot of conflict can be avoided by reliable and timely communication of information. Using an online calendar that you both can access easily and edit and making sure the other parent has all the same information as you do (either online or via paper or email) can help. Similarly, making sure you are both on pertinent email threads about the children can help avoid the "surprises" that lead one of you to feel marginalized (and possibly respond accordingly). You can also have a place online where you share common information such as sports schedules, clothing sizes, and contact information for doctors, tutors, and coaches.

Getting out of the unhealthy patterns of conflict and focusing the way you would in any other important relationship can help you depersonalize the objections of your co-parent and decrease your own tendency to blame or criticize the other parent. Your anxious or avoidant attachment needs, which we discussed earlier in this chapter, may have been very prominent. Letting go of the unhealthy attachment as you grieve the end of the marriage can be helpful, freeing you from the dynamic of spouses and allowing you to simply be the loving parent you are.

Wrapping It Up

In this chapter, we discussed attachment and how it plays out between co-parents and relates to conflict in your co-parenting relationship. Understanding the different patterns of conflict, and which ones are common in your relationship, will help you learn how to change the patterns so that they can be healthier, even if your co-parent is not willing to do so. Also, viewing your co-parenting relationship from the perspective of a business model can help you redefine your relationship and attend to your co-parent's strengths rather than flaws. And always keep in mind that you can gain control over the conflict even if you are doing it alone.

Taking It Home and Making It Yours

❋   Remember, unhealthy attachment can come from your background and what you learned early on about relationships. You can work to change your reactions and contributions to these patterns that often lead to hostility and conflict.

❋   Name the dysfunctional patterns so they are easier to spot. Plan and practice alternative responses in advance so you can quickly go to them in the midst of interactions with your co-parent.

❋   Try to stay focused on the parenting decision at hand, not who is right or who is to blame.

❋   Redefine your role as *parents*, not as "exes."

❋   Use technology to communicate basic information in order to prevent misunderstandings.

CHAPTER 7

Loving Your Kids More Than Loving the Fight

What did you feel the first moment your infant was placed in your arms? Many people describe a pure love, like nothing they have ever felt before. With few exceptions, as parents, you are the two most important people in your children's lives. You share the pride and joy of your children. You share their successes, and you share their challenges. You see them when they are cute and adorable—and when they're at their worst. You share an understanding about your children that others might just not get. You also worry over things large and small. They've captured your hearts.

Regardless of issues and differences between you and your co-parent, as profound as they may be, the two of you are connected as parents who will love the same children for the rest of your lives. This is a unique connection that persists, even if the love between the two of you has ended (or perhaps was never there in the first place). By honoring this shared love for your children, rather than getting embroiled in your issues with one another, you can keep your children in the spotlight and avoid countless hours of arguing and conflict. In this chapter, we will discuss how to stay focused on the bond created by your love for your children.

Child-Centered Co-parenting

When you are in conflict as parents, you tend to interact from your vantage point of being "right" and justified. You criticize your co-parent and defend against such criticism when it comes your way. You are often convinced that your positions are better, fairer, and more justified.

On the other hand, you can put aside your conflict and focus on making a decision from the standpoint of keeping your child's experience and well-being central to the point at hand. If, for example, your child wanted to go with your co-parent to see a newly released movie that they shared an interest in, you would figure out how this could occur, without getting into a struggle. You might exchange overnights or flex the routine schedule so your child could see the movie (without forgoing other important responsibilities). You might just say "sure" without flexing the schedule (as if your child were seeing the movie with a friend's family). It would be a matter of just making it happen, rather than it being a transaction based on what happened last time or what one of you or the other thought was "owed" or fair.

Co-parenting Fundamentals

The concept of co-parenting (two parents working together to help their children grow and thrive) works best when you work together as a team. We are fond of saying, "You don't have to like, trust, or respect one another to do the most important job of parenting." But of course, it helps. Even if you disagree on many parenting issues, you likely share at least some core parenting values, just as two teachers may have different classroom styles but share some core values regarding teaching techniques and helping students.

We have seen many instances where one parent sets the standard for co-parenting (as mentioned in chapter 5), even if the co-parent is not willing to work together in a more effective manner. When it comes to co-parenting, the question "What is the sound of one hand clapping?" (or just one parent working on improving his co-parenting behavior) can be answered with the statement, "It is a child experiencing a life that has less conflict in it." While it is best for both of you to focus on co-parenting, if only one of you does so, or you both do independently of the other, that is still preferable to neither of you taking the high road simply because the other won't. In short, it is difficult for your co-parent to engage in a conflictual interaction if you refuse to get brought into the conflict. By holding on to the co-parenting fundamentals described below, you can stay centered and know that you are giving your children the experience of having less conflict in their lives. This is not easy, so it is necessary to keep in mind and return to these co-parenting fundamentals when challenges arise.

Set the Standard

You can be the example of "best practices" when it comes to co-parenting. One way to make this happen is to remember that you are responsible for your own behavior (and your co-parent is responsible for hers). The thought I *was provoked to react this way* gives away your sense of self. No one can force you to respond a certain way. You have nothing to prove to the other parent, and you are probably not going to convince the other parent you are right simply by taking an angry or aggressive stance on an issue (or most likely by any means). Instead, you can resolve that your behavior (even when provoked) will be at the highest level (chapter 5). In other words, you don't have to take the bait and get drawn into an argument or retaliate against the other parent's offenses. You can respond to requests that are directly related to the children's needs and not about your failings, personality, or mistakes. By setting the standard, you can make sure that you are not sinking to the lowest level of communication possible, matching that of your co-parent. Concentrate on being the example of healthy communication.

Communicate About the Children (Not Each Other)

Communicating about the children is about (1) the sharing of information, (2) logistical planning, (3) making decisions, when possible, that set policies that will be common in both residences or relate to the children's lives (e.g., doctor's appointments, tutors, extracurricular activities), (4) exchanging input about the children, and (5) discussing what the children need to grow and thrive. These five areas form what we call a "ladder" of communication skills, as they all build on the ones that come before. The sharing of information is the easiest type of communication, while discussing what the children need to grow and thrive is the most difficult. Notice that these areas do not involve what either of you is doing wrong, what happened in the past, or either of your personality flaws. They involve working to make sure the communication itself has integrity and is not conflictual.

Keep the Children Out of the Middle

Children find themselves in the "middle" in so many ways. They can be "messengers" communicating from one parent to the other. Or, they can be asked (directly or indirectly) to keep secrets from one of their parents. They can be asked to judge one of you by being told about your actions or character. They can be required to choose between you simply by being asked who they want to be with. Putting children in the middle can cause them to feel as if they are betraying one parent or the other. It can cause them to feel as if they are "objects" to be traded back and forth. Ultimately, keeping them out of the middle avoids the control battle between you and your co-parent and allows the children to be free to love each of you.

Don't Get Stuck in Options

Parents often argue about two options as if one is clearly in "the best interests of the child" and the other is harmful. In our experience, the argument is usually about two viable options. Even in intact families, when parents and children agree about a decision (such as what sport a child will play this season), there are times when it does not work out. No one really knew what would be best. They just all thought they did. Rarely do parents pick options that are harmful for children. Instead, they argue about two reasonable options, both thinking they are right.

Sometimes agreeing to try one option and then shift to another, or simply accommodating the request of your co-parent, can be better than arguing for hours or days over what might be a small, one-time change in the transition time or a decision about one of two possible activities.

Affirm Your Children's Love for the Other Parent

Children should be free to love both of their parents. You can reinforce this value by allowing your children to have pictures of your co-parent at your residence, speaking respectfully to your co-parent when the children are with you, watching your body language when you are interacting with your co-parent in your children's presence, helping your children buy a birthday or holiday gift for their other parent, and showing that you respect your children's love for that parent by being civil, polite, and respectful in your communication. This also affirms your children's sense of self by supporting the validity of their feelings toward their other parent.

Exercise 7.1: My Co-parenting Fundamentals

In addition to the five fundamentals of co-parenting described above, there are others that you may find central to having healthy and productive interactions with your co-parent. Spend a few minutes and list the three most important behaviors or concepts you can return to whenever needed to help guide your response when you have a co-parenting challenge.

Attending to the Love, Not the Conflict

It is so easy to get distracted by your co-parent's personal attack or disregard that you experience. Yet that is a decoy that shifts your (and your co-parent's) attention away from the central job of caring for your children. Imagine if instead of attending to the conflict, disregard, or hostility, you attended to your mutual love for the children.

Let's look at the following scenario. The parenting plan states that the children shall return to you by 7:00 p.m. on a given night. Your co-parent wants to keep the children out later by thirty minutes. Your co-parent leaves you a message that says, "I'm sure you will be the usual selfish person that you always are and will not allow it, but I am going to bring them back thirty minutes later tonight. I don't care what you say. That's when the movie lets out and we are not leaving before it ends."

"Wow! What nerve," you say. There are so many traps and distractions in this short message that is just three sentences long. First, it begins with the insult "usual selfish person you always are..." It then moves on to declaring (rather than asking) that the children will be brought home thirty minutes later. It continues with the demeaning and disregarding statement, "I don't care what you say." Many of your peers, your family members, and even your therapist and lawyer might say, "You can't let her get away with that." You might be inclined to write back, "You don't get to make that decision. Who do you think you are? You are required by court order to bring the children back at 7 p.m., and if you don't I will call my lawyer!" What would you expect as the next reaction? Are you likely to get compliance? Or, are the children likely to hear that you prevented them from seeing the movie and being with their other parent? Are the children likely to be protected from the conflict, or thrown into the middle of it?

Here's another option. If you attend simply to the love and not the conflict, as difficult as it might be, you could ignore the bullying tactics and the insult. Instead, you could write back, "I know how much you love to be with the children and how important the movie series is to all of you. That's fine. I'm sure the children will enjoy it. Have fun!" This response protects the children from the conflict and keeps you from being engaged in a battle around the thirty minutes—a battle that could rage on over the next many days. Although you'd hope that this response would have a positive impact on your co-parent's subsequent behavior, it is likely that someone who interacts like that in the first place will continue to do so regardless of how you respond in this one instance. Your response is not about changing your co-parent. It is about avoiding pointless conflict that only can have a negative impact on your children.

Exercise 7.2: Detoxifying the Messages

Take the last hostile email or text message you wrote to your co-parent about a situation related to your children. If you were writing it now, how might you have detoxified this message? What kind of response did you get from your co-parent? Did she strike back and respond in anger? Did she avoid responding at all? Now look at the last hostile message you received about a situation related to the children. Look at your response. Was it a fight or flight response? Now, create a response that is simply about the children and your co-parent's love for them. As artificial as it may seem, what might the outcome have been if you had made this response? Would there have been as much hostility present around the issue, or would it have dissipated and resolved more quickly? It is pretty hard for your co-parent to pick a fight with you if you don't take the bait. You are in complete control of what messages you send. Can you be mindful of your own messages and seek to detoxify the communication between you?

Increasing Interpersonal Effectiveness

You may find that it generally is easy for you to get along with others. You may have difficult conversations with friends, business associates, and family, but you move beyond these rough spots effectively. However, this may not be the case with your co-parent. Do you find you get stuck and that even the smallest decision can seem like a burden to get beyond? Let's now focus on strategies to boost your skills when dealing with your co-parent.

Let's use an example. You and your co-parent are both caring and loving parents. You live in separate towns fifteen miles apart. Your ten-year-old daughter, Tina, played soccer last year in your town league. The season is about to start, and she said she wasn't sure she wanted to play this year. She said a lot of the kids on the other team are bigger than she is, and she was often out of breath on the field when running back and forth. Today, your co-parent calls and informs you that he signed Tina up for soccer in his town, since she played in your town last season. You are concerned about this unilateral decision, which may be in opposition to what Tina wants and may even be a medical issue given her complaint of being out of breath during the games. You bring it up and immediately hear, "Why do you always have to micromanage and control everything? I spoke to Tina about it and she said it was fine to sign her up. It's done."

What are your options? It can be difficult to avoid slipping into your familiar cycle; however, getting used to the strategies below can help give you other options. They may help you solve the problem, or at least stay calm.

Stay Focused on Your Child

It is really easy to slip into the conflict here. You have all but been called a "control freak" and told you have this intense need to micromanage everything. Yet your co-parent completely made this decision on his own, without seeking any input from you. Then, he told you, "It's done." If you move toward trying to show your co-parent the hypocrisies here, you will now likely be in a war of words over who did what to whom, and when it started.

Instead, we would recommend ignoring the first part of the statement. There is probably no way to answer the question "Why do you always have to micromanage and control everything?" in a way that will lead to some sort of understanding, agreement, or resolution. In fact, we would suggest it is not a question at all, but rather name-calling masquerading as a question. In other words, if he phrased it as a statement, you would have heard, "You always have to micromanage and control everything." Whether this is true or not, it is your co-parent's statement about *you*. That does not make it true. Unfortunately, though, it is not likely you will change your co-parent's opinion by saying otherwise. The parenting issue here isn't about your personality, or more specifically, your co-parent's view of your personality. It is about whether Tina is going to play soccer this season. Staying focused on Tina, not your co-parent's view of you, can help you avoid the conflict.

Don't Blame or Judge

After getting beyond the name-calling, your reaction might be, "You did what? How could you? We have joint decision making and joint custody. You don't get to make this decision on your own. What do you think you're doing?" This reaction is also one of blame. Perhaps one difference is that now the blame has switched direction. It is now coming from you and pointed toward your co-parent. However, either way, judgment, blame, and criticism are likely to cause a response that is either fight, flight, or freeze (see chapter 3). It keeps you focused on each other, and not on Tina.

It is so easy to resort to blame and judgment when you are criticized. However, it is so very important not to do the very same thing that upset you and was not helpful in the first place. In a moment, we will look at what to do, but first let's look at one more thing to avoid.

Avoid Reacting Emotionally

Stay calm and even-keeled. Use the skills you have learned in this book to breathe, quiet your ego, and control your thoughts and reactions. You need your logical mind to operate here. While the statement seems to be about you, the situation is not about you. It is about your daughter Tina. And it is not an emergency. Unless she has a very serious medical condition leading to her shortness of breath, she will probably be all right if she plays or does not play soccer.

Take a Time-Out

Because the situation is not an emergency, you do not have to respond right away. If you are not ready to deal with it now, or if you think your co-parent is not in a good frame of mind, you don't have to address it the moment it comes before you. You can always say, "Let's talk about this [specify another time]" without saying why. Offering the reason usually provides more opportunity to argue, as now there can be an argument about the validity of the reason for the delay.

Understand Your Co-parent

Many times you may have little true understanding of why an issue is important to your co-parent. In this example, it would be very easy to believe that what is important here is for your co-parent to prove to you that you are not in control and that he is. Tina playing soccer in the other town is a way your co-parent seems to have exercised control. It is obvious. Or is it?

While this could be the reason, there could be other factors at play leading your co-parent to make this decision. Typically, most parents don't stop to consider these other factors. Most don't say in a nonjudgmental way, "Help me understand why it is so important that she plays in your town." While you might hear, "Because you made the decision last year," you might also hear, "Because it is hard for me to get to the practices on time when they are in your town. I want to be an assistant coach, and there is no way that can happen, given the time I get out of work, if she plays in your town, which is even farther from my job." You can of course decide not to believe it, but what if, instead, you chose to believe what you heard? It would speak to a different motivation (not an excuse) for his unilateral decision.

Let's look at the conversation so far:

You: I understand you signed Tina up for soccer in your town.

Co-parent:	Why do you always have to micromanage and control everything? I spoke to Tina about it and she said it was fine to sign her up. It's done.
You:	(*without taking the bait, blaming, or reacting emotionally*) I understand and I'm not complaining about that (*making it clear that this is not a gripe*), though I'd like to understand why it is so important to you that she plays in your town.
Co-parent:	Why is it so important? I'll tell you. Last season I barely got to any of her practices. You know I work about forty minutes away from your town. I can't get out of work so early when she has an afternoon practice. I want to be an assistant coach, and I can't if she plays in your town. So I thought I'd just sign her up in my town, take Tina out of the middle, and just make it happen without an argument. Why should it matter to you?

By understanding what is important to your co-parent, you have a chance to support it. It is pretty hard to argue with someone who is saying, "I support what I understand is important to you." However, in this example, there is still more "bait" in the last question, "Why should it matter to you?" Here again, you can ignore the opportunity to get into conflict. Instead, you can focus on offering a bit of support by saying, "Wow. I think it would be great if you could be Tina's assistant coach. I know she would like that a lot." Of course, you could also mention that Tina complained of being out of breath, and that this is something you should both keep an eye out for in case she needs medical input.

Identify the Problems

In this relatively simple example, there are a number of problems (aside from the tone and name-calling and issue of where Tina plays soccer). We have identified the following:

1. Co-parent's desire to be an assistant coach without it interfering with his work schedule

2. The uncertainty of whether Tina really wants to play

3. Getting Tina to and from games and practice if she does play

4. Tina's complaints of being out of breath during the game

5. Unilateral decision making around extracurricular activities

There may be other problems too, but for the sake of this example, let's focus on these five. Once the problem or problems are identified, effective co-parenting communication involves the next four skills.

Stay Focused on the Present and the Future

Many parents would get distracted by discussing what happened last season, who made other decisions unilaterally, and which one of them has the moral high ground. They would get angry and critical of each other. This would just rev up the conflict and in all likelihood, be upsetting to Tina if she heard her parents arguing about soccer.

Instead, stay focused on the present and the future. What needs to happen with regard to this decision? Looking at the five problems with regard to this issue, we can view them all as related to the present or the future. Let's see what happens if we don't attend to what either parent said or did in the past. How you state the problem is very important, as it helps direct you to options (see below).

Bring In an Expert

When creating options, there are times an expert may be needed. In this case, a medical consultation may be needed to determine if Tina's being out of breath as she is running up and down the field is normal or whether it is perhaps an indication of a medical problem, such as asthma. An expert opinion can help when parents have different opinions on something about which neither one is an expert. You might need to make sure the expert is someone whom you both agree to consult; otherwise, you may need a second opinion if one of you disqualifies the opinion of the expert.

Raise the Issue to a Policy

Active day-to-day co-parenting can go on at least until a child is eighteen-years-old, and sometimes even longer. Many situations reoccur. It is important to have policies in place to address challenges so they don't become repeating problems. While policies may not always be followed, they can be the default to help address recurring situations. When you suggest a policy, it should specify the situation and apply to both you and your co-parent. In this example, there could be a policy that, going forward, before each season, you and your co-parent will discuss extracurricular activities and make a joint decision.

Create Options That Solve for "And" Not "Or"

Problems are solved by creating options that work for you both. Most arguments are win or lose. The choices are binary. You will do it this way *or* the other way. This leads to control battles, tug-of-war, and stalemates, all creating more conflict.

Instead of framing the discussion as an "or," we think it better to solve for the "and." By that, we mean taking into account *both* co-parents' views and priorities on the issue. Let's take the five problems above associated with this issue and address each one. We won't make any of them more important than the others. Instead, we will solve for "and" by addressing them all. Below, we will simply offer an option to address the problem. We know that in real life it may be more complicated; however, we are simply trying to show how this way of responding can help create more effective communication and problem solving, and also hopefully decrease the tendency for conflict. Certainly, if this was your situation, you might come up with other options as you work to create a response to your co-parent on this issue.

1. *Co-parent's desire to be an assistant coach without it interfering with his work schedule.* This can be a good thing and something you can easily support.

2. *The uncertainty of whether Tina really wants to play.* This needs to be determined. Tina might be uncomfortable saying what she really feels if she thinks there could be conflict between her parents on this issue. It might make sense to meet with her jointly and have a short conversation about it. When you do so, you both can say, "We want you to play if you want to, and not play if you don't want to. We both will support your decision either way." You also could let her start with the joint understanding that if she does not seem motivated, you will discontinue her participation.

3. *Getting Tina to and from games and practice if she does play.* This may be an issue on days when you are not able to stay for practice and Tina has to return to your home. Perhaps your co-parent would be willing to bring Tina home on these days or change the weekday parenting schedule during soccer season.

4. *Tina's complaints of being out of breath during the game.* This may need a medical assessment (bringing in an expert).

5. *Unilateral decision making around extracurricular activities.* A common policy (making joint decisions in the future) might make sense here, especially if your co-parent's perception is that you often have to be in control. Notice we are saying the *perception* of the co-parent, not necessarily the facts.

Combining the above five points into one statement, we get something like the following: "I think it would be great if you could be Tina's assistant coach (problem 1). I don't have an issue with her playing in your town, if we can address some other pieces of this. I'm not sure Tina really wants to play. I'd like us to sit down with her together and tell her we support whatever she wants, and then ask her (problem 2). Also, I'm thinking on practice days when she is supposed to be with me, we might want to change the overnight schedule, or would it be possible for you to bring her to me if I can't stay for the entire practice (problem 3)?" It would probably make sense to pause and see what the responses are to these areas before going on to the next two by saying, "I don't know if she mentioned it to you, but Tina said to me she was out of breath a lot. This of course could just be normal from running up and down the field, but I'm thinking we (notice the *we*, not *I*) just might want to mention it to her pediatrician (problem 4). Lastly, in the future, let's make sure we plan out each activity together before each season. I agree these should be decided jointly, not by either one of us (problem 5)."

This may seem a bit tedious. It certainly can be. That's why taking a time-out or planning your remarks before the discussion can be good ideas.

Exercise 7.3: Developing Options

Now, apply this same strategy to a situation you are dealing with. Find and print a recent email between you and your co-parent or write down on a sheet of paper or in your journal the problem at hand around a recent issue that was conflictual. Cross out the unessential, critical, or judgmental points. Then, list the problems and your co-parent's priorities as well as your own. Next, create options to address each problem or priority. Last, put it all together as a draft response to your co-parent. Fine-tune it so it reads smoothly; it's less likely to be interpreted as blameful or judgmental, and your co-parent just might see the support in your response. Perhaps you can notice the difference in this response compared to what you actually (or would have likely) said.

Interpersonal effectiveness is hard work, especially in difficult and challenging relationships. It is important to take your time and not respond out of habit or instinct in the moment. Keeping your logical mind active can go a long way to having more efficient and less conflictual interactions.

Creating Co-parenting Policies

Many times, parents argue over whose strategy is right. For example, they get in a battle over whether children should do their homework right after school or later in the day (especially if there are plenty of missed assignments reported by the teacher). They argue the pros and cons. They can seek experts' opinions and validate their positions by finding information online or talking to educators. Yet in this argument, they both share a common goal—the child should do the homework. What they really are not agreeing on is *how* to implement the goal. Here again is a major opportunity to avoid conflict if one parent says, "I agree wholeheartedly that homework is a major priority. While we don't necessarily agree about when it should be done in each of our homes, let's both commit to making sure it gets done each day so that there are far fewer missed assignments." The focus here is on reaching the goal, not the battle of which parent is right or how they will each reach the goal when the child is with them. By focusing on the goal rather than on the differing views around implementation, you can avoid getting lost in the weeds and arguing about something that will not be resolved.

This approach can be applied to many situations where there may be disagreement. For example, if there is a disagreement about bedtime on school nights, you could agree to a bedtime range that incorporates both of your views. The child could be told that bedtime is between (for example) 8 and 8:30 p.m. and that it is up to the parent the child is with on a given night. That gives each parent some flexibility and gives the child an understanding of the concept of the co-parenting policy. Most importantly, it avoids an extended battle between parents when the child is angling to stay up even later than 8:30 by saying to each parent that the other allows her to stay up later. By setting the standard together, each parent knows what has been put in place.

By setting co-parenting policies (agreeing on what will be common for the children between your two residences) you are increasing consistency about what you can agree on (rather than arguing about what you don't agree on). You also make it clear to your children that the two of you are "on the same page" on an issue and that you have communicated about it with a productive outcome (even if they don't like the decision that was reached). Your children will see that you are functioning as the "executive branch" of the family and feel that they indeed have two parents protecting and guiding them.

Such policy setting is also a useful strategy to take when it comes to one parent disappointing the other. It is easy to say, "You did something wrong." This often leads to counterattacks: "Why are you picking on me? I did something wrong? Well, what about when you did..." This cycle or pattern of discussion of course does not lead anywhere positive.

Instead, setting a policy has a better chance of leading to something useful. Rather than specifying who did what wrong, or defending against the criticism, it can be helpful to simply propose what the standard should be going forward. For example, let's say your co-parent did not tell you about a 64 your child got on a test. The school has a website, but you did not happen to check it on the day your child was with his dad. The following day, the child is with you, and tells you about a high grade he got in another subject but "forgets" to tell you about the 64. You praise and possibly reward him for the high grade. You subsequently find out about the lower grade from the teacher, who also tells you that Dad sent back the failing test paper with his signature. If you confront your co-parent about why he did not inform you of the 64, he is likely to say something such as, "I'm not your secretary. The school has a website. Why don't you just check it like I do?" On the other hand, he may respond more favorably if instead of criticism he hears, "I think it is important that we are both clued in to any low grades or academic concerns. Why don't we each let the other know if something comes up that is of concern, even if that info is on the website? That way we can both address it and make sure it does not slip by." This policy does not imply wrongdoing or poor co-parenting. It just simply addresses the behavior that may fix the problem going forward. By the way, your co-parent may also want to be aware of concerns that may or may not appear on the website.

When you put aside the need for emotional recognition and support, as well as parenting schedules and logistics, you can focus on where you and your co-parent can agree (rather than disagree). While each of you can be free to do more or less than the other with respect to the caregiving needed, perhaps you can set some co-parenting policies that can guide you both going forward.

Exercise 7.4: Establishing Co-parenting Policies

Draft some policies that may help the two of you rectify common problems. Be sure to word the policies so they apply to both of you and do not single out your co-parent in a blameful way. For example, you can think about different categories such as behavior and discipline, schoolwork, socializing, driving, and getting into other children's cars (for adolescents). Some other areas to consider are:

> What financial contributions to the well-being of the child (not specified in our divorce agreement) will we make together?

> When will we be present together with our child?

> What will our demeanor be with one another when we are with our child?

> How will we avoid making our child choose between us?

> When will we share information about our child with each other?

Are there any savings we want to jointly keep for our child (and possibly grandchildren)?

How do we want to address challenges when they arise? What will we do when our child does something serious that we don't approve of?

Will we work together when our child is faced with a major health, job, financial, or relationship challenge?

Should we jointly buy some holiday, graduation, or birthday gifts for our child?

Which parent is responsible (and when) if there is an unexpected change in the schedule (such as an early school dismissal)?

Write these policies down. It is quite possible that your co-parent might agree to at least some of them now and maybe others later. Paying attention to developing agreements can be so much more valuable than arguing about things where you are in disagreement.

Returning to Center—Following Ruptures with Repair

No matter how hard you try to avoid conflict, it is likely you will not always be successful. Sometimes you will have said something you think is neutral, or even positive, only to find that it "exploded" and was taken as the biggest insult. At other times, you may find that you slipped into conflict as you could not resist being provoked by what your co-parent said or did, or did not do. It is important to get back on the right track quickly (whether your co-parent joins you or not).

Here, apologizing can go a long way. While it may feel like you are admitting to wrongdoing, that is not the primary point. If you did not intend for your message to be an attack, or if you did not intend to allow yourself to be provoked, an apology can be a good first step to getting back on track. You can simply state, "I'm sorry we got off track here. I didn't mean for that to happen." Recognizing that there has been a rupture in your parenting relationship and making a practice of consistently following ruptures with repair will create a more solid foundation for your children.

If there has been a history of conflict, such statements may virtually be unheard of. In fact, sometimes parents joke that if they apologize, the other parent will fall over and faint (or they will if an apology comes their way). Yet the apology can, if nothing else, help you move forward and re-center on your core values around co-parenting. The apology can get you out of the traps of arguments and conflict and help you return to your own baseline of being the best co-parent you can be.

It's for Always

Your job as parents never ends. You are parents well beyond your children's eighteenth birthdays. In fact, in many ways, the job of being a parent to an older child can be more difficult. The risks to older children are greater (they can get into far more trouble and danger than young children) and the complexities of influencing and parenting older children also increase as your children move into adulthood. For example, helping a five-year-old transition into full-time kindergarten can be far easier than helping a twenty-one-year-old transition into living independently. Older children need their parents present and actively involved (although not necessarily daily). They need their parents to be able to guide them and communicate. The imperative for having a healthy relationship with your co-parent certainly does not diminish as your child moves into adulthood.

Deciding that the "war" is over can go a long way to giving your child many years of peace. The conflict of the divorce does not have to continue forever. Even if it was horrible at the outset, imagine how the years ahead can be better for your children and for you if you decide to stop engaging in bitterness and conflict toward each other. Imagine if instead, you commit to creating a family where you as parents hold on to the love and compassion you share for your children.

Wrapping It Up

In this chapter, we shifted the focus from you and your co-parent to your children. Making this shift gives the two of you a common goal of helping your children grow and thrive. Setting policies for your co-parenting relationship will make you the best team of caregivers you can be, now and throughout the lives of your children. Focusing on being present for your children is so much better than putting your energies into defending against attacks.

Taking It Home and Making It Yours

* Keep the communication with your co-parent child-centered. Even when you hear criticism, stay focused on decisions and plans related to your child.

* Connect with your co-parent on core values and co-parenting policies.

* Set the standard for the behavior you are looking for from your co-parent.

* Keep the children out of the "middle."

* Avoid conflict about reasonable alternatives.

* Affirm your children's love for their other parent.

* Focus on your co-parent's priorities.

* Apologize freely.

* Stick to the business of co-parenting.

CHAPTER 8

Divorce Recovery

Going through a divorce is for most people one of the most difficult times in their lives. This is normal and natural. However, divorce should not define your life. It is something that about half of all married couples go through. It signals the end of one important chapter in your life and the start of another. Recovering from the divorce allows you to move forward into your own future in a healthier way, with insight and hopefully as a more authentic you, who can be conscious and present in your future relationships. This last chapter provides some additional ideas about how to get from the misery of divorce to a place of recovery, which can enhance your life immeasurably and can also greatly improve your children's sense of well-being.

Staying on Course

It is so easy to get derailed and activated, yet so important to stay on course, soothe the part of you that gets activated, and recover quickly when you do get derailed. This lessens the impact of episodes of conflict on you and your children and allows you to spend more time and energy in other areas of your life, enabling you to create meaning and positive memories beyond the divorce. Learning skills of distraction, reassurance, and holding can go a long way to helping you stay on course.

Distraction

You can focus on the hostile email you received from your co-parent, responding immediately and addressing every false claim and misrepresentation to "set the record straight." This would be equivalent to watching the wind, rain, and lightning outside the window during a vicious summer storm. You can choose to sit there petrified of the next "thunderclap," or you can pull yourself away from the email, distracting yourself from the emotional provocation and get involved in almost anything else. There is no email emergency here. The tree is not about to fall on the house as a result of the storm. It is just a hostile email (perhaps one of hundreds). It can wait until later, and especially until you are operating from your centered self, in the right frame of mind to respond to it. We recommend that if you feel the need to respond immediately, you create a "do not hit send" policy and save your impulsive response in a separate folder to review at a later time when your centered self prevails.

Reassurance

Your co-parent is upset, hurt, and angry. She is not even-keeled. She is not okay. That is her experience. She strikes out at you, but that does not have to be your experience. You can say to yourself, *I'm okay. This is my co-parent's experience, not mine. I will handle this later when I figure out what I want to say and how I want to say it. There is no danger here—just anger. I'm absolutely okay.* This is the same reassurance you would give the child in the storm: "We're okay. The storm will pass and we can go outside (deal with the email) later. We're safe here."

Holding

This is a little more difficult than simply throwing your arms around yourself. However, it is not really all that complicated. In this context, *holding* means holding on to your center, or staying grounded. You can do this with rational thinking, breathing, and meditation. The idea is not to give yourself away to your co-parent's emotional state, but to hold on to your own sense of self and your own control.

Holding does not change your co-parent's behavior or complaints. It changes your reaction. It preserves your independence and unlinks you from his feelings, words, actions, and emotional state. It creates boundaries that separate and protect you.

You can still respond to your co-parent, but more from a place of healthy detachment than unhealthy emotional connectedness. If you respond from a healthy place, you will be more emotionally available for your children and perhaps not slip into exacerbating the conflict or a difficult situation by your own reaction. So often the struggle between parents is worse (for them and the children) than either alternative they are struggling about. Why engage in the struggle when you can focus on remaining even-keeled?

To build these skills, take situations that are far less stressful, perhaps not related to co-parenting, and use distraction, reassurance, and holding. For example, let's use an example of being stuck in traffic. Practicing distraction would mean turning on the radio, appreciating the scenery, or thinking about your loved ones. Practicing reassurance would mean saying to yourself, *I'm okay. There's a lot of traffic, but it will eventually clear. I will pass the problem and get to where I'm going, even if I'm late.* Practicing holding could be done by breathing and settling down the physiological and emotional activation that was occurring.

With practice, many people find they can do this regularly in less stressful situations. Then, they can get better at using the skills in more stressful situations. These are skills that take time and repetition. You first need to learn the skills in less demanding situations before being able to apply them at more demanding times.

Forgiveness

How often have you heard friends, relatives, the clergy, and people in the media say, "You just need to forgive and move on?" That is one of those "easy to say, hard to do" expressions. It may even seem impossible. The person who inflicted the pain may not show remorse. He may not care if you forgive him and may continue to be hurtful, even years later, acting in mean and spiteful ways. To begin to practice forgiveness, let's first look at and try to understand it.

Forgiveness as Absolution

Common synonyms for the term *forgiveness* are *pardon, absolution, mercy,* and *amnesty.* These imply that the act of forgiveness is about the person who was hurt letting the other person "off the hook." It is as if you are saying, "If I forgive you, you no longer have to feel guilty for what you did to me." We experience this in everyday social situations when we say, "Excuse me" or "I'm sorry" and the other person says, "No problem" or "No worries." The other person has given us absolution of sorts, and we can go on with our day not feeling guilty for the (usually minor) hurt that we have caused. Even as a child, when we spilled something and said, "I'm sorry," our parent (in a healthy family) would say, "That's okay. Just try to be more careful next time." If the child was old enough, the parent would have the child "repair" the wrong by helping to clean up what was spilled. Even in more serious situations, the parent might say, "I am really disappointed in what you have done, but I love you." The parent may also help the child think of and plan a reparative action and demonstrate understanding of what the "injured party" felt. The message is "You are forgiven and you are okay." That allows the child the freedom to go from being uncomfortable or feeling guilty to feeling more comfortable or not guilty. In other words, the act of forgiveness helped the perpetrator of the misdeed to be free of guilt.

When we look at forgiveness in this way, it can be easy to wonder, *If I am hurt, why is it up to me to forgive—and help—the person who hurt me? I am the one who needs taking care of.* In this instance, forgiveness is a burden on the one who is hurt. The person who did the hurting is the one who gets the consideration. If you experienced a lot of pain in the divorce, forgiveness can feel like an impossible task, and in some ways, it is—when looked at in this way.

Instead, let's take a different look at the hurtful interaction and the thoughts and feelings related to it. Throughout this book, we have stressed that feelings are not just automatic responses to the situations we face. They are more often related to how we look at situations and what we tell ourselves about the situation. In other words, we hold on to our hurt, not because we have been hurt, but because we are unconsciously allowing ourselves to stick with it. This idea of holding on to something unconsciously (even when it is not about hurt) is illustrated in this well-known ancient Buddhist story.

Two monks are walking from one village to another. One is a wise old monk and the other is a much younger student of his. Generally, they walk in silence. They have taken a vow not to touch women, or even to make eye contact with them. As they approach a stream that runs between the villages, they see a young maiden who is distressed. She is very fretful, pacing back and forth. The older monk breaks his silence as he wants to help and says, "Madam, it appears that you are fretful. Might we be of help?" The woman explains that she is trying to visit her mother, who lives a good distance beyond the stream, but she is afraid that her clothes will be ruined if she tries to cross the stream (which is flowing with rushing water from the recent rains). The older monk suggests that he and the younger monk lock arms, making a sort of seat for her. He suggests that they can then, if she would like, carry her across the stream and place her safely on the other side so she can go on her way. She accepts their offer, and, after she is on the other side of the stream, they depart from one another at the next fork in the road. After they say their good-byes, the monks return to silence and continue their journey. Time passes and after a few hours the younger monk interrupts the silence, wondering if he might ask his mentor a question. The older monk says, "Of course," and the younger monk says, "You know, Father, I have been thinking, we have practices and vows not to be close to or touch women. Back at the stream when we locked forearms to help the maiden, we rolled up the sleeves of our robes and she sat down on our exposed arms. We not only were touching her, but we were of course touching her in an extremely personal way as her bottom was across our arms. How was it okay to carry her like that?" The older monk quickly answered, "We were being of help to her. However, I put her down on the other side of the stream and you clearly are still carrying her all this time later."

Unfortunately, in divorce, many of our "maidens" are the hurts that we have experienced. Not only don't they go away, but they reoccur, and often we don't let them go as we replay and retell the stories to ourselves and others, over and over again.

Forgiveness as Letting Go

The Cambridge dictionary defines "forgive" as to stop being angry with someone who has done something wrong. Notice how it has virtually nothing to do with the other person doing anything to repent. It has to do with the person who holds the anger (or hurt or resentment) stopping the feelings. If you wait for the other person to do something, then you are allowing your feelings to be dependent on the actions of the other person. The younger monk in the story does not need words from the maiden to "put her down"; he needs to figure that out on his own. He is the keeper of his thoughts.

Sometimes, you can get a little help if the other person earnestly apologizes, as the apology is often a cue to begin letting go of the hurt. However, in divorce, this usually is not the case. Often, an earnest apology is not forthcoming or, when it is, is difficult for a hurt or betrayed ex-spouse to accept. And often, more hurts occur in postdivorce life, especially after an adversarial divorce.

Even an apology from your co-parent in one area may not undo the hurts that have continued to occur in other areas. And what if the apology is not forthcoming, or, as we mentioned in chapter 3, what happens if the person you are upset with is yourself? In our view, forgiveness should not and cannot be dependent on the actions of someone else. It is up to you. It is not something that just happens with the passage of time; people can hold resentment and grudges for decades. Forgiveness is an internal action that requires consciousness, intention, and a shift in your heart. Unfortunately, it is often quite painful, as we are weighted down by carrying the hurts for years (as if the young monk were carrying the maiden for miles and miles).

Our minds attend to the pain. And our minds can let go of that attention. This first of three exercises shows you a way to use imagery to help you release from the pain.

Exercise 8.1: Letting Go of the Hurt Through Imagery

List three ways your partner hurt you over the course of the relationship that still bother you today. Next to each one, jot down the approximate date when the hurt occurred. Note how long you have been carrying the hurt. How often do you think of these stories? How often do you tell them to others (therapists, partners, friends, and family)? What if you stopped reliving and replaying them? What if you put them down on the other side of the stream? What if they actually (unlike the maiden) flowed away in the stream? Next take a few moments and close your eyes. Clear your mind and then imagine writing each of the three ways you were hurt on a separate leaf. Imagine putting each leaf in the stream and letting it float out of sight. This is something you can repeat frequently until perhaps you don't feel the need.

The next approach involves a meditation.

Exercise 8.2: Letting Go of the Hurt Through Meditation

In this exercise, first, center yourself. Breathe slowly and rhythmically. When you are ready, allow the feeling of the hurt to come into your consciousness. Then, softly, with each inhalation, breathe in feelings of love and self-nurturance and forgiveness. And, with each exhalation, breathe out the hurt and resentment. Letting go is not about struggle or forcing something to happen. It is about *opening and releasing* the struggle. Keep doing this throughout the rest of the meditation, until you are ready to clear your mind again and just breathe comfortably before concluding. As with so many of the exercises in this book, this meditation may be something you decide to return to many times. Notice when you return to it what you feel and how the feelings may change over time.

You can add a writing component to the meditation.

Exercise 8.3: Letting Go of the Hurt Through Meditation and Writing

First quiet your mind. Breathe slowly and center yourself. Then allow yourself to focus on the three hurts you listed in exercise 8.1. Feel the extent of the pain and hurt and its impact on you. Perhaps envision it as a color or image of some sort. If you feel tears, allow them to flow, and when you are ready, open your eyes. Then write about the extent of the pain. Write at least two paragraphs about what you felt during the short meditation you just did. Write about why it hurts so badly—still. Seek to understand the meaning of the pain and why it is so hard to let go of. Lastly, give yourself permission to let go of the pain, to release it, to leave it in the tears and on the paper.

Forgiveness by letting go is not about pretending that the injury never happened or did not matter. It is not "no worries." It is not about simply *accepting* that it occurred. Rather, it is about acknowledging the full impact of the hurt and then releasing it, rather than being defined by it. It is as if you are saying, "I have been hurt badly by what happened, but I'm going to let go of it in order to move forward in my life."

GRACE

Putting down the hurt and resentment is a step toward letting go of the pain. It can help you feel less burdened and be less reactive to your co-parent's repeated offensive behaviors. However, while putting down a burdensome weight can bring you back to neutral, so to speak (that is, how you are when you are not holding the weight), it does not bring you from the negative position of holding the weight to something positive. To do this, we believe it is important to go forward even further—five steps further. To help you remember these steps, we have taken the first letter of each and spelled the word GRACE (Gratitude, Respect, Acceptance, Compassion, and Equanimity). Let's look at each one. We have touched on these throughout the book but are going to put them all together here.

Gratitude

Are you aware of deep feelings of gratitude toward your co-parent? Most people we speak with are not. They say, "Are you kidding? Gratitude? How can I feel grateful for the mess my co-parent has put me and our children through?" They are right. We can't expect them (or you) to feel grateful for the "mess." However, what if you focus away from the mess? Remember, where your mind goes, your feelings follow. What if you start to focus on what you are grateful for?

Exercises 8.4: Gratitude

See if you can focus on what you can feel grateful for when it comes to your co-parent. Please list these in your journal. Here are some hints to get you started. See if these or others apply.

Helping you conceive or adopt your children

Providing income to help you care for the children

Providing direct caretaking of your children

Loving your children

Being a role model in certain areas for your children

Having stronger parenting skills in some areas than you do

Helping your children with extracurricular or academic activities

Making your children laugh

Of course, there are many other areas where you may be able to feel gratitude toward your co-parent. After you list them, leave some room in your journal to come back and add to the list from time to time. Refer to this list when you are particularly resentful of your co-parent, to shift your mind off of the resentment and pain and onto perhaps more important contributions your co-parent makes for your children.

The simple practice of gratitude can be another tool in your mindfulness toolbox. In your daily life, you can practice gratitude by simply thinking of at least one thing each day that you can be grateful for related to your life with your children. By searching through the day and looking for an experience, event, observation, or sensation that you can be grateful for and reliving that moment, you are cultivating mindfulness. Despite the challenges you may have getting along with or co-parenting successfully with your parenting partner, there are bound to be characteristics, interests, talents, and other aspects of her parenting that add value to the life of your children. It is helpful and worthwhile to spend some time focusing on these things, as they can help you shift your mindset and can profoundly influence your state of mind.

Exercise 8.5: A List of Qualities I Appreciate in My Co-parent

Make a list of your co-parent's characteristics, interests, talents, or other factors related to parenting that add value to your children's lives.

What did you find when you worked on this list? Were you surprised by your responses? Did you find that there weren't enough lines for you to write on, or were you unable to think of even one thing to say? If this is the case, try to dig deep, thinking about what qualities you loved or valued in your co-parent when you first met, and when your children were born. Was there a time that you could have filled this list? What would your responses have been then? Has the anger and pain of betrayal obstructed your ability to recognize anything positive about your co-parent's connection to your children?

Once you have gotten in touch with some of the value your co-parent brings to the lives of your children, write this on your list.

In preparation for developing a deeper practice of gratitude, we would like you to prepare to write a thank-you note to your co-parent. You may find that what you wish to express thanks for is providing a wake-up call to you to help you grow, move forward with your life, and develop a more authentic self. Or perhaps you will find that you are thanking your ex-partner for valuable and meaningful experiences, support, your children, your lifestyle, redefining yourself, or any other positive aspect in your life. Whatever you find, it is helpful to reflect on it. Perhaps something will emerge that surprises you.

Exercise 8.6: A Thank-You Note to My Co-parent

(This exercise was developed by Jenny Douglas for her Grief and Gratitude workshop.)

Set a timer for five minutes and write a thank-you note to your co-parent. Write freely, without evaluation or judgment. You can write either in a narrative form or as a series of independent sentences. If you choose the latter, begin each sentence with "Thank you." You may focus on concrete things that your partner provided in the marriage, on your lifestyle, aspects of parenting, your children, experiences you had together, or qualities in your partner that you see and value in your children. Perhaps you will focus on ways in which the breakdown of your marriage helped you to grow. Once you have written your note, give yourself some time to sit and reflect on what you wrote. You may wish to read it aloud to yourself, or to share it with a trusted friend. Let yourself experience whatever comes up for you in this exercise. It can be quite powerful to hear your own voice reflecting on what you are grateful for in the relationship with someone who will always be in your life and the lives of your children.

Respect

When most people speak of respect, they are referring to holding the character of the other person in high esteem. You often hear, "Respect is earned, not given." We don't think this view is very useful in difficult divorces. Rather, we think respect is *given*, not *earned*. Respect is not about your view of the *character* of your co-parent. It is about your *behavior* toward your co-parent, your willingness to treat her in a respectful manner, regardless of her character. In many ways, it is about *your* character.

For example, let's say a stranger comes up to you and asks for directions. He seems to be from another country and barely speaks English. He is not dressed particularly well and has not revealed much of his character to you at all. Based on your first impression, you might feel a little standoffish. If you treat the stranger harshly, is that a reflection of the stranger's character or your own? If you treat the stranger with respect and dignity, is that a reflection of the stranger's character or you own? We think both circumstances reflect your character, not the stranger's.

Imagine applying this concept to your co-parent. What if you behaved in a respectful fashion? Are you acknowledging his character, or are you validating your own? We think behaving respectfully is more a sign of your own character and your respecting your children's love for their other parent.

Exercise 8.7 Respect

Think of all the types of interactions you have with your co-parent (such as regarding a transition or schedule, or at a child's event or other family function). List some ways you can offer respect in those situations. By the way, this is not about looking for some better outcome from your co-parent. In fact, your co-parent may think you are faking or may have a hostile response to your respectful behavior. The point here is not how your co-parent reacts. It is about how you react and consequently feel about your reactions. To help you with this exercise, consider the earlier example about the stranger asking for directions. If you were disrespectful to the stranger asking for directions, how would you feel? How would you feel if you provided directions in a respectful way? Rely and build on the list of respectful actions you can take toward your co-parent.

Acceptance

In this context, acceptance is about recognizing and not trying to change the traits of your co-parent. We are not saying that the traits that bother you are fine and are just your problem. Rather, we are saying that your co-partner's traits are hers. If you did not like your co-parent's height, it wouldn't change because you didn't like it. Neither will her personality characteristics and behaviors change because you find them hurtful or annoying. So much energy in a marriage goes into each person trying to change the other in some way by saying things such as, "Why won't you do what I am asking of you? How many times do I have to ask?" This does not lead to change. If it did, couples would remain blissfully married, as all they would have to do is verbalize what they wanted the other to do for the other to be the ideal partner. In divorce, couples continue this pattern of criticism and judgment, as if it could lead to change in the other person.

Acceptance is recognizing that your co-parent is as he is. It is seeing that this person is the person he is and is not likely to change in the way you want him to simply because that is what you want. We would even suggest that at times some of the traits you don't like in many circumstances might be traits that you are grateful for in other circumstances. For example, if your co-parent is stubborn and rigid and won't back down on something, you might find this really annoying. However, the same trait can come in handy when you both are advocating for your child to get special services from the school and your co-parent won't back down.

Exercise 8.8: Acceptance

List three to five annoying traits of your co-parent. Next, write in your journal about each trait and under what circumstance it might be a strength or come in handy. Then close your eyes and meditate by focusing on your breath and allowing your thoughts to float by like leaves in a stream. When you are ready, think of your co-parent. Offer acceptance as she is, including these traits. For example, you might say, "I accept you with your rigidity. That is part of all that you are." You can then add, "And, I accept that I cannot change you, and I need to co-parent with you, as you are." Part of the acceptance is the realization that you do not have a choice here. That is, you can only deal with your co-parent as she is, and not as your idealized version of who she is. Your co-parent too, whether she recognizes it or not, has the same challenge, as you can only be who you are, not her idealized version of you.

Compassion

No one has a monopoly on pain. We all have it. In divorce, both people usually feel pain. They may not feel it for the same reasons and may not even share the same perceptions of what contributes to the pain or who caused it. But they both feel it. Unfortunately, they often don't see it in the other. Rather, they say things such as, "What's wrong with you? Why can't you see what you've done to me and our children and how you've hurt us all?"

Compassion is about seeing the other's pain and humanity. You do not have to agree with what or who caused it, and you don't have to measure it against your own pain (to prove who has more). It is just about having a consciousness about the other's distress and a desire for the other person's distress to be alleviated.

If you desire your children's other parent to be in pain, that is probably about wanting vengeance of some sort. However, it does not help your children to have a parent in pain. In fact, it more than likely does the opposite. That is, if your co-parent is in pain, it probably leads to more conflict and to some reduced parenting capacity when your children are in his care.

Can you imagine wanting your co-parent to be as strong and as healthy as possible? Can you imagine honoring your children's love for their other parent and setting a standard for well-being throughout the family? If you knew your co-parent had pain from a serious illness, might you offer compassion? We would like to suggest you do the same for your co-parent's emotional pain (regardless of the cause).

Exercise 8.9: Compassion

In your journal, write to your co-parent a compassionate wish for healing. Then meditate by clearing your mind and breathing calmly and easily. After you are centered, repeat the compassionate wish for healing to your co-parent in the meditation. Feel free to later repeat this wish silently when you are interacting with your co-parent and you see his pain surfacing through his (possibly hostile) words and actions toward you or the children. Perhaps at some point you can even offer compassion aloud to your co-parent by your words or actions.

Equanimity

Equanimity means remaining calm, even-keeled, and level headed. As we discussed earlier in this chapter, maintaining equanimity in the face of adversity is, even in life-threatening situations, something that can help you avoid a flight, fight, or freeze response (see chapters 1 through 3). It enables you to respond fully to the situation without the emotional panic (even if you feel scared, hurt, or angry) that can lead to poor judgment or be disabling. Remaining even-keeled is not something you learn to do in a high-stress time or in the face of an emergency. Rather, it is something you learn to do step by step in far less stressful situations. It is based on the learnings and practices throughout this book and involves combining your breathing with your rational thinking.

Exercise 8.10: Equanimity

There are times of adversity and stress when you may be aware of an inner calmness: a deep sense of knowing what you need to do in that situation, a deep sense of clarity. Take your time and get centered in a meditation. Focus on your breathing and allow your mind to become clear and quiet. See if you can allow that sense of clarity to connect with your consciousness. See if you can tap into that "knowing." Pay attention to how it feels, and to the comfort that comes from that centeredness. Then later, when you are not meditating, experiment with remembering that feeling. Call on it when you are not stressed. When you can easily remember it, start calling on it at times when you are mildly stressed (perhaps in a long grocery line), and then when you are more and more stressed, so that you can return to it when needed.

We hope that the skills, teachings, and meditations we have shared with you throughout this chapter will help you effectively deal with the challenges of high-conflict divorce and postdivorce parenting and moving forward with your own healing and transition. We view the concept of GRACE as the embodiment of peace and centeredness. Even if the storm rages outside, it is about staying in touch with your love, compassion, and centeredness for the sake of your children and your own soul.

Wrapping It Up

This last chapter focused on some final steps toward recovery, beginning with strategies of distraction, reassurance, and holding, and then on to forgiveness. The additional skills and concepts encapsulated in GRACE (Gratitude, Respect, Acceptance, Compassion, and Equanimity) help you remain centered and be your most authentic self as you go forward with love, hope, and compassion for yourself and others.

Taking It Home and Making It Yours

* Remember there are few actual emergencies. Reassure yourself that you can get through the challenge of the moment.

* Give yourself the emotional support and holding you need.

* Forgive your co-parent *and* yourself as quickly as you can.

* Acknowledge what you are grateful to your co-parent for.

* Offer respect to your co-parent.

* Accept your co-parent, strengths and limitations in all.

* Offer compassion to your co-parent, who is in pain too.

* Remain even-keeled, keying into your centered core.

Closing Thoughts

Yes, divorce is certainly a life-altering, stressful experience. Whatever course your journey takes, you can be sure that life won't be the same as it was. Your life, and that of your co-parent and your children, will be changed. We hope that through your journey you will find the principles and teachings that we have addressed helpful to you. Stay centered. Avoid the repetitive patterns of conflict. And recognize that others (especially your co-parent) don't define you—even if they are being critical.

We hope, as you go forward, that your divorce becomes just one of the many stories of your life, and that over time it drifts away from the center of your attention, allowing your self-love and love for your children to dominate your day-to-day experience as you move onward with peace and with GRACE.

Acknowledgments

We are grateful for the wonderful support we had from our team at New Harbinger, from Wendy Milstine, who was instrumental in developing the concepts for this book, to Ryan Buresh, Nicola Skidmore, Clancy Drake, and Vicraj Gill. We are deeply grateful to Rona Bernstein for her masterful editing of the final manuscript. Her understanding of our material and sensitivity in the editing process was indispensable. We had a great experience collaborating with all of them as we wrote and edited. Their input was extremely valuable and helped shape this book from the initial idea to its completion.

We also want to acknowledge all of the parents and children who have entrusted us with their pain, shared with us the darkness of their conflict, and taught us so much about what helps and what hurts.

References

Bowlby, J. 1969. *Attachment and Loss.* Vol. 1, *Attachment.* New York, NY: Basic Books.

Brach, T. 2003. *Radical Acceptance: Embracing Your life with the Heart of a Buddha.* New York, NY: Bantam Books.

Brown, B. 2012. *The Power of Vulnerability: Teachings of Authenticity, Connection, and Courage* [audiobook]. Louisville, CO: Sounds True.

Campbell, J. 2008. *The Hero with a Thousand Faces.* Vol. 17. Novato, CA: New World Library.

Cohen, G. L., and D. K. Sherman. 2014. "The Psychology of Change: Self-Affirmation and Social Psychological Intervention." *Annual Review of Psychology* 65: 333–371.

Goleman, D. P. 1995. *Emotional Intelligence: Why It Can Matter More Than IQ for Character, Health and Lifelong Achievement.* New York, NY: Bantam Books.

Hicks, D. 2011. *Dignity: The Essential Role It Plays in Resolving Conflict.* New Haven, CT: Yale University Press.

Johnson, S. 2008. *Hold Me Tight: Seven Conversations for a Lifetime of Love.* Boston, MA: Little, Brown, and Company.

Johnson, S., and A. Sims. 2000. "Attachment Theory: A Map for Couples Therapy." In *Handbook of Attachment Interventions,* edited by Terry M. Levy. San Diego, CA: Academic Press.

Kabat-Zinn, J. 1990. *Full Catastrophe Living: Using the Wisdom of your Body and Mind to Face Stress, Pain, and Illness.* New York, NY: Delta Trade.

Kübler-Ross, E. 1969. *On Death and Dying: What the Dying Have to Teach Doctors, Nurses, Clergy, and Their Own Families.* New York, NY: Scribner.

Lesser, E. 2008. *Broken Open: How Difficult Times Can Help Us Grow.* New York, NY: Villard Books.

Linehan, M. 1993. *Cognitive-Behavioral Treatment of Borderline Personality Disorder.* New York, NY: Guilford Press.

McKay, M., and A. West. 2016. *Emotion Efficacy Therapy.* Oakland, CA: New Harbinger Publications.

Ricci, I. 1997. *Mom's House, Dad's House: Making Two Homes for Your Child.* New York, NY: Fireside.

Siegel, D. J. 2009. "Mindful Awareness, Mindsight, and Neural Integration." *The Humanistic Psychologist* 37(2): 137–158.

Siegel, D. J. 2010. *Mindsight: The New Science of Personal Transformation.* New York, NY: Bantam Books. Kindle edition.

Siegel, D. J. 2012. *Pocket Guide to Interpersonal Neurobiology: An Integrative Handbook of the Mind.* New York, NY: W.W. Norton & Company.

Thayer, E. S., and J. Zimmerman. 2001. *The Co-parenting Survival Guide: Letting Go of Conflict After a Difficult Divorce.* Oakland, CA: New Harbinger Publications.

Winnicott, D. W. 1960. "Ego Distortion in Terms of True and False Self." In *The Maturational Processes and the Facilitating Environment: Studies in the Theory of Emotional Development,* edited by Donald W. Winnicott. London, England: Karnac Books.

Lauren J. Behrman, PhD, is a clinical psychologist with over thirty-three years in independent practice helping adults, children, and families work through transitions. She has evaluated and treated children and families since 1976 at Schneider Children's Hospital, Nassau BOCES, and as chief psychologist at the Child Development Center of the Jewish Board of Family and Children's Services from 1985-1994. Behrman completed her postdoctoral training in child, adolescent, and family psychoanalytic psychotherapy at the Postgraduate Center for Mental Health in 1990. She has taught and supervised doctoral candidates, was adjunct professor in the graduate psychology departments at Long Island University, Yeshiva University, and New York University. She is a frequent presenter, author, teacher, and trainer for professionals in Basic Collaborative Divorce Practice. Behrman is a founding partner of The Practice Institute and the Center for Advanced Professional Education at University of Redlands in Redlands, CA. She is in independent practice in New York City and Westchester County, NY. You can find Behrman on the web at www.lauren behrmanphd.com, and can read and subscribe to the authors' blog and newsletter at www.mydivorcerecovery.com.

Jeffrey Zimmerman, PhD, ABPP, is a licensed psychologist with offices in New York City and Westchester County, NY, and Connecticut. He has over thirty-five years of experience working with families and individuals experiencing the stress of separation and divorce. He is coauthor of articles on divorce, as well as two related books: *The Co-Parenting Survival Guide* and *Adult Children of Divorce*. Zimmerman received the Distinguished Contribution to the Practice of Psychology Award from the Connecticut Psychological Association for his work with high-conflict families of divorce. He is trained as a mediator, parenting coordinator, and collaborative divorce professional. He is a frequent speaker, trainer, and mentor of other professionals and graduate students. He is also founding partner of The Practice Institute. You can find out more about Zimmerman on the web at www.jeff zimmermanphd.com.

MORE BOOKS *from*
NEW HARBINGER PUBLICATIONS

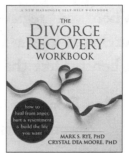
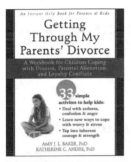

Register your **new harbinger** titles for additional benefits!

When you register your **new harbinger** title—purchased in any format, from any source—you get access to benefits like the following:

- Downloadable accessories like printable worksheets and extra content

- Instructional videos and audio files

- Information about updates, corrections, and new editions

Not every title has accessories, but we're adding new material all the time.

Access free accessories in 3 easy steps:

1. Sign in at NewHarbinger.com (or **register** to create an account).

2. Click on **register a book**. Search for your title and click the **register** button when it appears.

3. Click on the **book cover or title** to go to its details page. Click on **accessories** to view and access files.

That's all there is to it!

If you need help, visit:

NewHarbinger.com/accessories

new harbinger
CELEBRATING
40 YEARS